INTRODUCTION

Introductions generally try
to lead a reader to some understanding of the book in hand.
Calling this page an introduction contributes to
the illusion that what you are holding is a book,
and that you are in fact a reader.
What you are holding is nonsense,
or at least the illusion of nonsense.
When you are able to make some sense
of the words and pictures herein, consider yourself
clever and witty and exceedingly good-humored.
And when you are not, consider the answer section.

CONTENTS

GAMES
MAGAZINE

THE BOOK OF
SENSE
AND
NONSENSE
PUZZLES

Edited by Ronnie Shushan   Designed by Don Wright
Workman Publishing, New York

Games magazine sense and nonsense puzzles.

Includes index.
1. Puzzles.   I. Shushan, Ronnie.   II. Games.
III. Title: Sense and nonsense puzzles.
GV1493.G29 1985   793.73   85-40528
ISBN 0-89480-930-X (pbk.)

Cover design by Bill Jensen and Tedd Arnold
Cover illustration by Akio Matsuyoshi
Back cover illustration by Dave Calver; typography by Dave Herbick

Workman books are available at special discounts when purchased in bulk for
premiums and sales promotions as well as for fund-raising or educational use.
Special editions or book excerpts can also be created to specification. For details,
contact the Special Sales Director at the address below.

Workman Publishing Company, Inc.
708 Broadway
New York, New York 10003

Manufactured in the United States of America

First Printing October 1985

10   9   8   7   6

The material in this book has previously appeared in *GAMES* and *The Four-Star Puzzler*,
which are trademarks of Playboy Enterprises, Inc.

What do these items have in common?

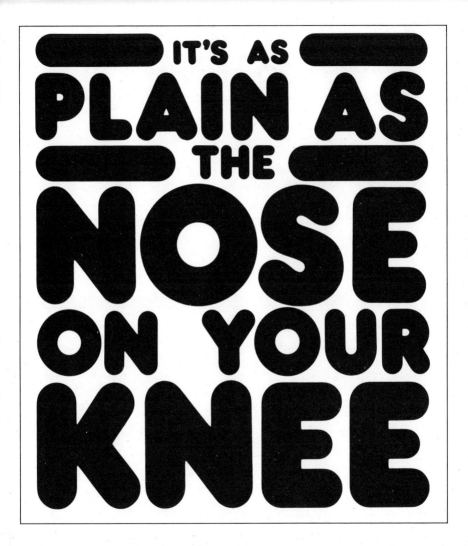

ONE NEVER KNOWS, DO ONE?

In this battle of wit, there's more than one way to skin a cat.

1

Can you connect the dots with the shortest possible line?

●   ●

2

Can you move one match to make a perfect square?

3
What is the next number in this series?

3   **6**   **9**   **12**   _____

4
Complete this simple crossword.

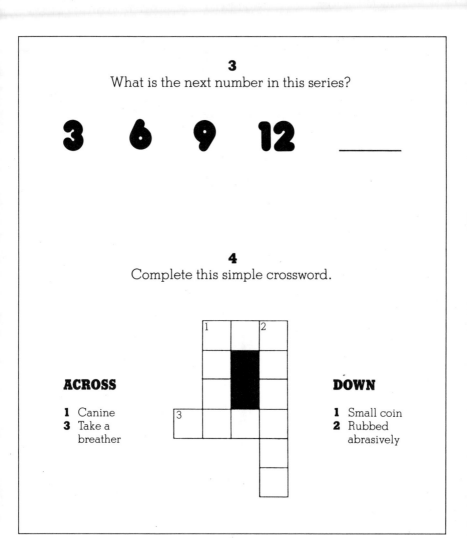

ACROSS

1 Canine
3 Take a breather

DOWN

1 Small coin
2 Rubbed abrasively

DROODLES

Roger Price, who invented Droodles in the 1950s, calls them dopey little drawings that don't look like much of anything until you know the correct title. For example, the drawing below, at left, could be A Mother Pyramid Feeding Her Young. It could be, but it's not. How do you know? Because the title says it's A Ship Arriving Too Late To Save A Drowning Witch. The drawing at right is much more straightforward; unless you turn it 90° counterclockwise and find, alas, A Deceased Trombone Player. Can you give an appropriate title to the Droodles on the following pages?

A Ship Arriving Too Late
To Save A Drowning Witch

Man Playing Trombone
In A Phone Booth

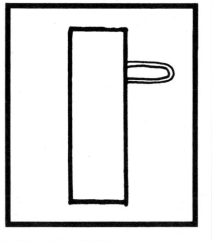

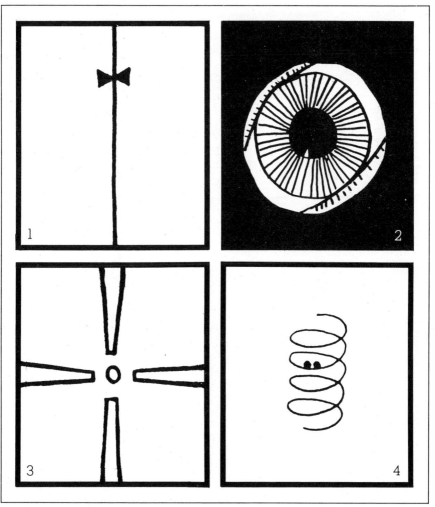

11

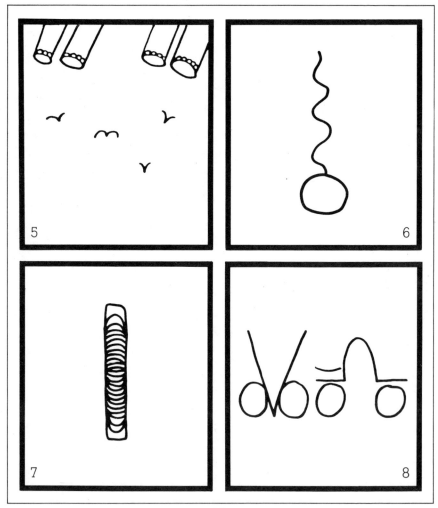

9

14

THREE TEASERS

In the trio below, we mean what we say—if you know what we mean.

1

A bus with no passengers stops, and five people get on. At the next stop eight people get on. At the next stop six people get off. How many people are on the bus?

2

You are seated next to the pilot of a small plane at an elevation of one mile. Huge mountains loom ahead. The pilot does not change speed, direction, or elevation, yet you survive. How?

3

It is noon. You look at a clock. The big hand is on the three and the little hand is on five. What time is it?

UNCOMMON EQUATIONS

How can 6 + 24 = 1?
When 6 days are added to 24 hours to make 1 week, that's how.
Can you solve these other uncommon equations?

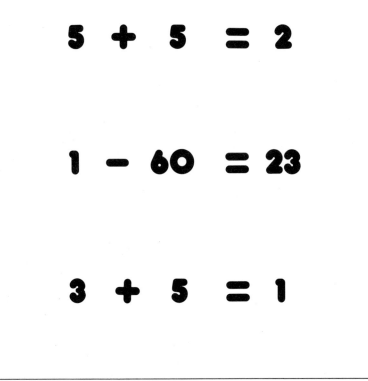

$$5 + 5 = 2$$

$$1 - 60 = 23$$

$$3 + 5 = 1$$

TIC-TAC-TOE

Which line wins this game of tic-tac-toe?

ELASTIC APTITUDE TEST

The Elastic Aptitude Test (EAT) has been designed to measure the distance your imagination can stretch. Unlike traditional aptitude tests, which reward a humdrum command of facts, EAT rewards Flexible Agile Thinking (FAT). Also unlike traditional aptitude tests, parts of EAT have been scattered throughout the book, so you have to find the test before you can take it.
Now then, how flexible is your mind?

PART I: MATH

Can you make these numbers make sense? Calculators are permitted.

1
3 is to 9 as 4 is to _____
a) 10   b) 12   c) 16

2
Two cards are drawn at random from a standard deck. What is the probability that they form a pair?

3
86 is to 98 as 73 is to _____

4
Which of the following numbers is divisible by 3?
a) 34   b) 29   c) 55   d) 102   e) 7

5
What are the next three terms in the following series?
1, 3, 5, 7, ___, ___, ___

WACKY WORDIES

Little typographic word pictures, like the ones printed here, began arriving in the GAMES mail in 1979, and readers have continued to send them to the magazine ever since then. The object is simply to discern a familiar phrase, name, saying, or cliché from each arrangement of letters and/or symbols. For example, number 1 depicts the phrase "Trafalgar Square," and number 2 shows "eggs over easy." Easy enough so far. . . .

1

T R A
F A L
G A R

2

eggs
easy

3 sɪɪky *(upside down)*	**4** ʇɐǝl wǝu *(upside down: new leaf)*	**5** ᴘᴀ**INS**
6 $\dfrac{\text{L} + \text{O}}{\text{SS}}$	**7** league	**8** D U C K
9 or O or	**10** pit	**11** wheel wheel drive wheel wheel

23

12

told told tales
told

13

swear
bible
bible
bible
bible
bible
bible
bible
bible

14

bridge
water

15

set one's teeth

16

-attitude

17

power

18

Wilson

19

tr ial

black

20

L
Y
I
N
G
JOB

21

prosperity

22

E R C
  T N U O

23

century

24

writer's

25

✓ ✓ ✓
counter

26 **me snack al**	27 **hoppin**

28 **busines**	29 **bet one's** **dollar**	30 **tpmerhao**

31 **2 par** **t** **o** **n**	32 **orseman**

33 way yield	34 rifle rifle rifle rifle rifle rifle rifle rifle	**school**
36 what must		35 37 price
38 dictnry	39 everything pizza	

27

WHAT ARE THE RULES OF THIS PUZZLE?

In solving any puzzle, the most important thing to remember is to follow the rules very carefully. The rules of this puzzle may not be as concise as those of other puzzles in this book—but to compensate, we've made the task required by the rules very easy.

Each rule of this puzzle is written as a sentence. The fact that one sentence precedes or follows another does not, in itself, give either sentence priority over the other. Every sentence ends with a period that looks like this:. The sentences are grouped into paragraphs, each paragraph separated from the next by a space. This sentence, for example, is in paragraph number two. The order in which the paragraphs appear on these pages, however, does not necessarily correspond to their numbers. For instance, the paragraph that appears next is paragraph number five.

You should ignore any sentence in this paragraph that begins with the word "ignore." Ignore the previous sentence, if you dare. If two sentences in the same paragraph contradict one another, follow the one that comes last. But if two sentences in the same paragraph contradict one another, follow the one that comes first.

The name of this puzzle is: "What is the name of this puzzle?" The answer to the puzzle is the name of the puzzle and a single two-digit number. The two-digit number referred to in the last sentence must be formed by writing together the numbers of this paragraph and the paragraph that appears last in these rules. And, in case you've forgotten, the name of this puzzle is: "What are the rules of this puzzle?"

This paragraph takes precedence over all others. The last sentence in the next-to-last paragraph of these rules is to be ignored. (The following sentence takes precedence over all others in this paragraph except for any that are in parentheses.) For the purposes of the second sentence in this paragraph, the order of these paragraphs is not to be considered the order in which they appear on these pages, but rather the order in which they are numbered, as determined by the rules. For instance, for numbering purposes, this is really paragraph number one. The paragraph that appears immediately before this one is paragraph number six; it has an error in it. In order to interpret the rules of this puzzle correctly, you must correct the error by substituting the word "adding" for the word "writing." Or rather, you must correct the error by substituting the word "multiplying" for the word "writing."

The paragraph that appears first is really paragraph number three. Ignore the rest of this paragraph, except for the next sentence. The number of this paragraph is either two, four, or six. If this is paragraph number five, then the name of this puzzle is "No-name" regardless of anything that may be said elsewhere in these rules. Ignore this sentence and the next. Don't ignore the previous sentence. Do ignore both this sentence and the previous two.

THE
EVEN-IF-YOU-HATE-SPORTS
SPORTS QUIZ

If you think that Abdul-Jabbar is an OPEC nation, that the draw
play was invented by Picasso, and that clutch refers only to cars,
don't despair. This little quiz was designed to show just how
much you *do* know about team sports . . . in spite of yourself.
As for you hard-core sports fans, don't assume that
all the answers are gimmes.

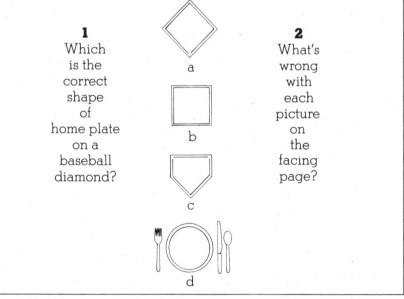

1
Which
is the
correct
shape
of
home plate
on a
baseball
diamond?

2
What's
wrong
with
each
picture
on
the
facing
page?

FROM THE FLIMFLAM FILE

In building up a puzzle file over the years,
Martin Gardner created a special folder for short
problems whose answers are based on
some sort of joke, swindle, misdirection, or other
kind of flimflammery.
You're forewarned, but how many of his
questions will still trip you up?

1
Explain the meaning of this acronym:
ETMOTA

2
What letter is exactly in the middle of the alphabet?

3
What's the opposite of "not in"?

4
A deaf and mute man and a blind man entered a hardware store
together. The deaf and mute man indicated to the clerk that he
wanted a saw by pretending to saw a piece of wood. The blind
man wanted a pair of scissors. How did he make the clerk
understand what he wanted?

5
The blind man in the previous question was with a friend on a
hunting trip. The friend hung the blind man's hat over a
projection, the blind man walked 100 yards away, turned
around, and easily shot a bullet through his hat.
How did he do it?

6
Which would you prefer—that a lion ate you or a tiger?

7
Irrational numbers such as π and the $\sqrt{2}$ are said to be
NEVER ODD OR EVEN.
What's so remarkable about that description?

8
You throw a die 20 times and it comes up 5 on 17 out of 20
tosses. What's your best bet for the next roll?

9
Tennis players and bowlers wear sneakers; football players wear
shoes with cleats. In what sport are the shoes made
entirely of metal?

10
Punctuate the following couplet to make it rhyme:
There was an old farmer and he
Was deaf as a post.

11
What unusual word of seven letters has three U's in it?

12
One class has seven times as many boys as girls. Let b stand for
boys and g for girls. Write the equation that expresses the ratio.

13
How many animals did Moses put on the ark?

14
Said a carpenter to his assistant
"Dawitcanooseeeyeoteyeoutullaails?"
What was he trying to say?

15
How do you keep a moron in suspense?

When asked their names, a dozen boys answered at once, and
they were photographed just as each one was beginning to
pronounce his own name. The 12 names were Oom, Alden,
Eastman, Alfred, Arthur, Luke, Fletcher, Matthew, Theodore,
Richard, Shirmer, and Hisswald. Can you lip-read each face in
this class portrait and identify each boy correctly?

34 Answers, page 149

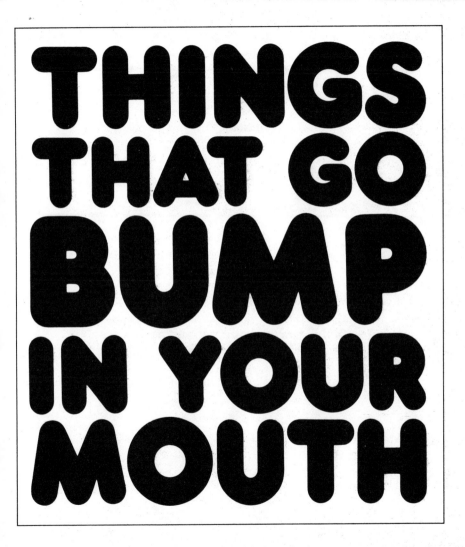

SATE WITH SCOTCHOGRAMS

A Scotchogram might be defined as a puzzler's way
of sending a telegram and saving money.
By combining the sounds of two or more words
into a single word or coinage,
the sender creates a message that must be deciphered
before it can be understood.
And he saves money by reducing the number of words
in the message.

Consider this exchange between two workaholic puzzlers.
The first wires:
HYACINTH YOU EDIFICATION?
The second responds:
MINERVA'S WRECK. MUSCATEL AUTO HERE.
(Translation: "How are you since you had a vacation?"
"I'm a nervous wreck. Must get the hell out of here.")

Can you decipher the Scotchograms that follow?
Go ahead, TRITE. You CONDUIT.

1
OMNIVEROUS HAPPY SIAM VENOM WITH YOU DEAR.
LOVE ENCASES.
2
CANOE SPEND THIS WEAKEN WIDOWS ENOCH
COUNTRY? WIRE DEMENTIA KNOW.

3

DOUGHNUT BATON THE RESOURCES. AVOID TO DEVISES SUFFICIENT.

4

ALBEIT DETRACT. UNIVERSE EDIFY MUSTAFA TICKET TICKET IN.

5

WENDY HOUSECOAT FIRE, SCIATICA MATADORS INJUSTICE SAXON SHORTS.

6

WEARY TURNING DISORDER SYNTHESIZES SARONG.

7

WEED LICHEN ICE CHEST FOREARM OTHER. DISGUISE DELIMIT.

8

CANCEL MYOCARDIA. ITS INFORMAL FUNCTION.

9

YEARN AFFIX. LOST UKASE. UGANDA JAIL. CONSERVE TENURES. YACHT APPEAL.

10

BOB STILT SEA. CANTANKEROUS BOAT. HUMUS GOAD IMMORTAL DECOS GUARD.

11

EYELET SHEILA INDIA HOUSE. SHEILAS TURKEY.

12

MARY SINBAD. SHEER TOURNEY. AUGUSTA WIND NOCTURNE TOOTHBRUSH.

13

WHINE YOSEMITE NAMES SOY CAN PHILATELIST?

EYEBALL BENDERS

The challenge here is twofold. First identify the 10 objects. Then sound out their names in order, from photo 1 to photo 10, to decode the message they form. When you're done, you will have identified the two qualities necessary for solving this puzzle.

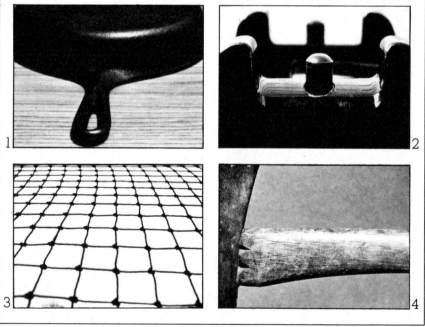

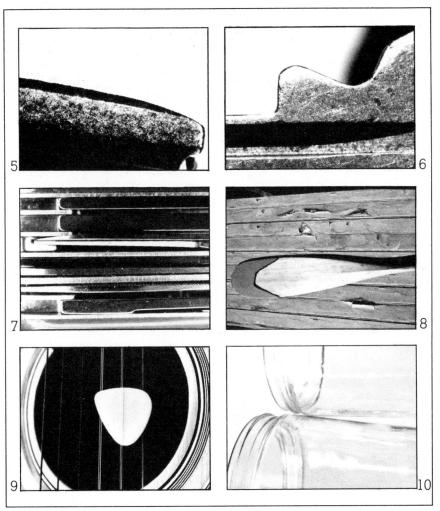

BO'S BEAUS' BOWS

Each clue below defines a set of
three homophones—words that sound alike
but are spelled differently.
For example, "Mrs. Derek's boyfriends' neckties"
would be "Bo's beaus' bows."
Can you solve them?

1
Golf warning to quartet

2
Understood novel wildebeest

3
Consider milk-part method

4
Peel fruit duo

5
Stop precipitation rule

6
Scribble ceremony correctly

WILLIAM MARRY ME?

Remember knock-knock jokes? Someone comes up to you and says, "Knock knock." You say, "Who's there?" and he says, "William." You say, "William who?" and he says, "William marry me?" In this variation, we supply the last part of the answer; you fill in the blank with the right name to make the joke work. For example, "_____ poor Yorick" could be completed with "Alice."

1
_____ lace is untied.

2
_____ wall carpeting is too expensive.

3
_____ any questions from the audience?

4
_____ body home?

5
_____ Welk can do it, so can I.

6
_____ the tub. I'm dwowning!

MARRIED WOMEN

When *Star Wars*
was first the rage,
a joke circulated that went
something like this:
If Ella Fitzgerald married Darth Vader,
her name would become
Ella Vader.
Similarly, in these puzzles
you are first given a clue
to the
identity of a famous woman,
followed by a clue
to her proposed mate,
and then a clue
to the humorous married name
that she would have as a result.
(In the world of puzzle jokes,
wives always
take their husbands'
last names.)
As with "Ella Vader,"
the pronunciation of the answer
may be approximate.

1

If an actress named Miles married a noted consumer advocate, she would become a singer of love songs.

2

If an actress named Lupino married a Hawaiian singer, she would become a source of potatoes.

3

If the Kennedy mother married the title character in a Melville novel, she would become a sign of spring.

4

If a female outlaw named Starr married a star of the movie *The Paper Chase,* she would become a variety of pants.

5

If the star of *10* married a long-time singer-actor-vaudevillian, she would become a bunch of flowers.

6

If the star of TV's *Maude* married the star of the movie *Superman,* she would become "deprive by death."

7

If TV's Bionic Woman married the male lead in *Charlie's Angels,* she would become an ingredient of varnish.

8

If Sigmund's daughter married the composer of the Hungarian Rhapsodies, she would become a practitioner of the profession originated by her father.

CARTOON REBUSES

These picture puzzles are solved by sounding out various elements of each picture. The answer to each one is the name of a person, place, or thing, and is found by combining any or all of the following elements:

■   Words or synonyms of words spoken by the characters or found elsewhere in the picture
■   Names of objects in the picture
■   Isolated letters in the picture
■   Words implied by the cartoon's action or scene

These elements are combined *phonetically* to form a name fitting the clue above the cartoon, which gives the category of the answer followed by the number of letters in the answer.

The example at right depicts a magazine with a two-word title: six letters in the first word, four in the second. The answer, *Vanity Fair,* is found by combining VAN, the object pictured in the background; the word IT spoken by the cabbie; the letter E on the van; and the word FARE, suggested by the scene. Put them together phonetically and you have VAN-IT-E-FARE. Can you figure out the others?

Ex. Magazine: 6, 4

1 Zodiac Sign: 6

2 World Capital: 7

3 Fictional Character: 8, 6

4 TV Show: 2, 9

5 Entertainer: 6, 7

6 Country: 6

7 Baseball Player: 6, 4

8 Annual Occasion: 5, 3

9 Song: 3, 4, 4

SH-BOOM!

Okay, all you bobby-soxers
and be-bop big daddies,
name the golden oldies
in which
these memorable scats appear.

1
Fe fe, fi fi, fo fo, fum
2
Oo ee oo-ah-ah, ting tang walla-walla bing bang
3
A-bop bop a loobop, ba lop bam boom
4
Oohwah, oohwah, oo-oo waah, oohwah
5
Lincoln Lincoln bo bincoln banana fana fo fincoln
6
Doo-lang, doo-lang, doo-lang
7
Imminy maa-maa-maa, imminy maa-maa-maa
8
Yip-yip-yip-yip-yip-yip-yip-yip, boom-oom-oom-oom-oom-oom
9
Dom doobie doo dom dom, comma comma
10
Doo-run-di, rundi rundi, baba doo-run

AD INFINITUM

Below are 10 famous advertising slogans in which all the major words are represented by their initials. For example, "P. D. S. the C." would stand for "Please don't squeeze the Charmin," while "Y. D. a B. T." would be McDonald's "You deserve a break today." TV ad-dicts may have an ad-vantage in solving.

1
The A. E. C.—D. L. H. W. I.

2
L. Y. F. D. the W. through the Y. P.

3
G. to the L. D.

4
P. a T. in Y. T.

5
P. P., F. F., O. W. a R. I. I.

6
W. Y. C. E. to S. the V. B.

7
R. O. and T. S.

8
H. Y. D. a F. L.?

9
F. the F. S. of U.

10
A. Y. G. Y. U. D.?

BLPS

Can you
solve
this one
without getting tongue-tied?

EVERY BLIP IS A BLOP.
HALF OF ALL BLOPS
ARE BLIPS.
HALF OF ALL BLEEPS
ARE BLOPS.
THERE ARE 30 BLEEPS
AND 20 BLIPS.
NO BLEEP IS A BLIP.

Therefore,
how many blops are neither
blips nor bleeps?

SIMPLE ADDITION

Add up the numbers below by reading each new total aloud, like this: one thousand, one thousand ten, two thousand thirty, etc. Do *not* add by totaling the individual columns in the usual way. Sounds easy, doesn't it?

1000

10

1020

10

1030

10

1010

10

OMPHALOSKEPSIS...

Here is a crossword for any time you just want to relax and contemplate your navel. Several people we know have solved it without vanishing.

ACROSS

1 See 1-Down
5 The party line
10 See 46-Down
14 See 2-Down
15 More capable
16 See 11-Down
17 See 3-Down
18 ___ Janeiro
19 See 12-Down
20 Locale for a stead?
23 Oolong and peppermint
24 Stop bleeding
25 ___ for an eye . . .
28 Famous Peer
31 Room
32 Locale
34 African madman
35 Put on the payroll
36 For ___ sake
38 Modern fabric
39 Circus animal
40 Clothes with authority
41 Coke, for example
44 Sheltered (from crossword clichés?)
46 Niche for a slot?
53 See 47-Down
54 Port of Rome
55 See 50-Down
56 See 48-Down
57 Plural of faux pas?
58 See 51-Down
59 See 13-Down
60 Precious few
61 See 52-Down

DOWN

1 Leave immediately, wretched cats!
2 Money
3 Italian wine region
4 Room for a salon?
5 Amu ___, river on USSR–Afghan border
6 Last words, of a sort
7 Radiate
8 French wine region
9 Pertaining to square measure
10 Cubbyhole for dens?
11 See 53-Across
12 See 56-Across
13 Famous flagmaker
21 An adolescent (see also 46-Down)
22 Gear parts
25 "Pa's ___": Palindrome
26 58- and 59-Across, e.g.
27 Typewriter type size
29 Sedaka and Armstrong
30 Mystical deck
33 Cubbyholes
37 Niche
38 Stove part
42 City on the Rhône
43 Soc. or org., perhaps
44 Par ___
45 Fewest
46 These, in British dialect; or, with 21-Down, a number significant to the lady in 13-Down
47 Leander was her hero
48 A flower (proving beauty is in the eye of the beholder?)
49 Recently active volcano (may ante up)
50 State on the Ohio
51 Chamberlain
52 Brief message

IS EASY

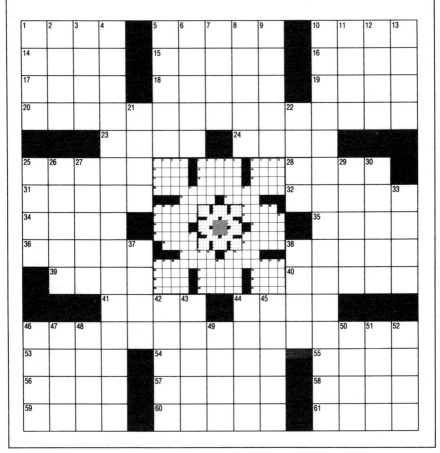

HOW'S THAT AGAIN?

If you understand news accounts of Supreme Court decisions, if you know how your aunt's second cousin is related to you, if you never get lost in a parking lot—then the following items will give you no trouble. If they do, welcome to the club.

The Supreme Court today reversed its earlier ruling that let stand an appellate court's decision to overturn a lower court's finding that a café owner had no right to fire a waiter for refusing to deny service to a male patron who was not wearing a tie and jacket. *If a male patron now enters that café without a tie and jacket, is he likely to be served?*

Jack: Remember that book you lent me? Well, I lent it to my mother, and she lent it to her sister, who gave it to her son-in-law, who thought his wife's maternal grandfather would like it. He did, and lent it to his wife, who gave it to her son John. Last night John dropped in and asked me to return it to his son. So here it is.—Jill   *How are Jack and Jill related?*

"Hi, Bill. Let's meet at my office, okay? The building's on the north side of Main. Turn left down the hall and take one of the elevators on your right as high as it goes. Across the hall there's another elevator. Take it to the 50th floor. When you get out, turn left and look for a door on the right that says UP. Go in, turn right up a short staircase, then turn left through the exit door at the top of the stairs. Walk down the hall that goes to your right, and my office door is on the left." *Which direction will Bill be facing when he knocks on the door?*

ELASTIC APTITUDE TEST
PART II: LATIN

Though it's no longer a requirement in most schools, Latin is far from being a dead language. Match each Latin phrase at left with the English translation at right.

1. bona fide

2. rara avis

3. sic transit

4. vice versa

5. id est

6. alter ego

7. vide supra

a. A good rental car is hard to find.

b. See the janitor.

c. Freudian self-actualization (see *alter ego*)

d. ambulance

e. Change your psyche. (see *id est*)

f. good dog

g. dirty poem

WHAT'S NEW?

The panels in this comic strip have been jumbled, making the punchline punchless. Can you put the panels in the single logical sequence that leads to the joke?

1 _____   5 _____

2 _____   6 _____

3 _____   7 _____

4 _____

by Robert Leighton

56

Answer, page 151

57

CONFUSABLES

Was it Charlotte or Emily Brontë who wrote *Wuthering Heights*?
Is an electron positively or negatively charged?
Was Alaska or Hawaii admitted to the Union first?
We've read or heard these facts so many times,
but still the answers often escape us.
In this quiz, a score of 10 for 15 is good.

1

Was Romeo a member of the Capulet family and Juliet a
member of the Montague family, or was it the other way around?

2

Your car battery has died and a friend hands you his jumper
cables. Do you connect the poles + to + and − to − ,
or + to − and − to +?

3

Between the *Lusitania* and the *Titanic,* which one was sunk by
an iceberg, and which by a German U-boat?

4

In a cave you notice rock formations hanging from the ceiling.
Are those stalagmites or stalactites?

5

Was Plato a student of Socrates or Socrates a student of Plato?

6

On a loom, is the series of lengthwise yarns known as the warp
or the woof?

7

At sea, your captain calls all passengers to the ship's starboard. If you are facing the bow, do you head left or right?

8

Copper and tin are melded to form a common alloy. Is that alloy brass or is it bronze?

9

Did Pocahontas marry John Smith or John Rolfe?

10

Between apogee and perigee, which is the high point of an orbit and which the low?

11

Of the *Monitor* and the *Merrimac,* which was the Union ship and which the Confederate?

12

If you need to be treated for an eye infection, should you see an optometrist, an ophthalmologist, or an optician?

13

Is the boiling point of water higher or lower at higher elevations?

14

Do four bushels of grain make a peck, or do four pecks of grain make a bushel?

15

At graduation ceremonies, do you shift the tassel from the right side of the mortarboard to the left, or from the left to the right?

CHOPLOGIC

To understand Choplogic, you first need a little refresher course in Logic 101. Remember Aristotelian syllogisms?

1 Drinking hemlock will make you get sick and die.
2 Socrates drank hemlock.
3 Therefore, Socrates got sick and died.

Choplogic is a direct offshoot of this Aristotelian brand of deductive reasoning in that the statements that make up each syllogism are true (or at least true enough for our purposes). Choplogic differs only in that one must occasionally make a nonsensical leap between statements. With this handy-dandy loophole, it's possible to prove virtually anything.

Why Elephants Are Wrinkled

1 Elephants live in Africa.
2 In Africa there are many bodies of water.
3 One kind of body of water is a pool.
4 To play pool, you use a cue.
5 Cues are what actors need for their lines.
6 Lines are wrinkles.
Therefore, elephants are wrinkled.

Proof that Sherlock Holmes Was a Detective

1 Sherlock sounds like "sheer lock."
2 A sheer lock is an invisible hair.
3 One invisible hare was named Harvey.
4 Harvey Kuenn managed the Milwaukee Brewers.
5 The word "Milwaukee" contains only one I.
6 An I by itself is a private I.
7 A private eye is a detective.
Therefore, Sherlock Holmes was a detective.

Why an Airplane Flies

1 The airplane was invented by the Wright Brothers.
2 Brothers are male offspring of the same parents.
3 Just off-spring is summer.
4 In summer there are lots and lots of flies.

Therefore, an airplane flies.

Why Cats Meow

1 A cat has whiskers.
2 Whiskers are hairs.
3 A hare is a rabbit.
4 A rabbit runs fast.
5 To fast is to go hungry.
6 To go hungry is painful.
7 When I'm in pain, I say "ow!" In other words, me "ow."

That's why cats meow.

Proof that There Is Life After Death

by G. Frank Crowell, winner of the GAMES Choplogic Contest

1 After a death, there is a mourning.
2 After the morning comes the night.
3 Past the knight is the bishop.
4 Beyond the bishop is the pope.
5 The pope has serious convictions.
6 After a serious conviction, you get life.

Therefore, there is life after death.

Proof that Snow Is White

by Alfred J. Brennan, Choplogic Contest runner-up

1 Snow falls from clouds.
2 Snow clouds are gray.
3 Gray is almost black.
4 Black is the color Zorro wears.
5 Zorro is an outlaw.
6 An outlaw steals money.
7 Money makes you happy.
8 Happy was one of the Seven Dwarfs.
9 The Seven Dwarfs lived with Snow White.
10 Snow White married Prince Charming.
11 Snow Charming sounds ridiculous, so she kept her maiden name.

Therefore, snow is white.

Can you turn this picture into a correctly worked division problem by substituting a different digit from 1 through 9 for each type of fruit?

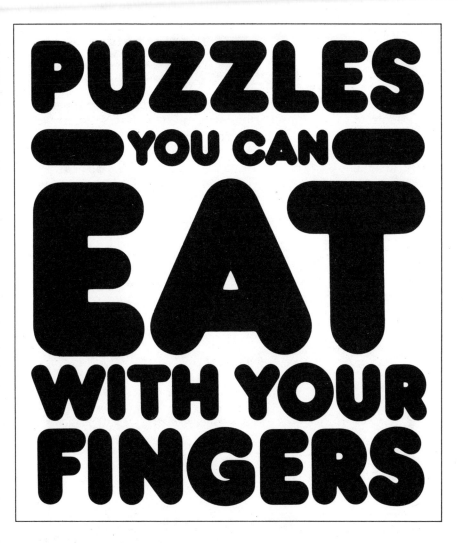

SUBSTITUTIONS ALLOWED

The proprietor of The Name Drop Inn has a very unusual menu.
Though it features mainly standard American fare, you have to
know your celebrities to understand what you're ordering.
Replace each underlined first name with the appropriate
last name and you'll be able to decipher all the dishes.
For example, in number 1, The Name Drop doesn't really serve
"mixed LORNE salad"; that's Mixed GREENE salad.
Can you determine the usual names for the rest of the dishes?

THE NAME DROP INN

Appetizers

Mixed <u>LORNE</u> salad
1

Prosciutto and <u>ANDREW</u>, in season
2

<u>SHIRLEY TEMPLE</u>   <u>ORSON</u> soup
3   4

Seafood

Broiled Alaskan <u>ALAN</u> <u>BUSTER</u> legs
5   6

Fillet of <u>VERONICA</u> trout
7

<u>ALISTAIR</u>'s special <u>DINAH</u> dinner!
8   9

Includes:

Shrimp steamed in the <u>MAXIMILIAN</u>
10

Home-made <u>HAMILTON</u> sticks
11

<u>NATALIE</u> slaw, corn on the <u>LEE J.</u>
12   13

Meat and Poultry

Sliced <u>JULIE</u> broil, <u>IRENE</u> as you like it
14   15

<u>ANN</u>-fried chicken
16

Pheasant under <u>RON</u> stuffed with <u>OSCAR</u> <u>JIM</u>
17   18   19

<u>CYBILL</u>'s pie
20

<u>FRANCIS</u> <u>WARREN</u>
21   22

on a sesame-seed <u>ESTHER</u>
23

with our delicious

hash-<u>HELEN GURLEY</u> potatoes
24

Desserts

<u>VIDA</u> <u>CHUCK</u> pie
25   26

<u>EZRA</u> cake
27

<u>JACK</u>–lime sherbet
28

Beverages

Selections from our wine <u>PETER</u>
29

Hot <u>JAMES</u>
30

Coffee or <u>MR.</u>
31

POETRY IN THE KITCHEN

A poet, opening a new restaurant, offered a special dish or drink to every guest on opening day. The first to arrive was Juan Carlos of Spain, followed by some friends from the American Legion. The poet chose a coffee ring for the king and chocolate eclairs for the legionnaires. Can you pick the dish or drink he offered to each of these other guests?

1. Queen Noor Al Hussein
2. Sandra Day O'Connor
3. Notre Dame's "Fighting Irish"
4. Prince Charles
5. a Turkish nobleman
6. three hobos
7. two Arab potentates and their harems
8. a few strikebreakers
9. a group of convicts
10. a church official and some sisters from the convent
11. Khomeini

a. mints
b. leeks and chives
c. lox
d. plums
e. granola
f. crabs
g. grenadine
h. liquor and buns
i. kasha
j. fudge
k. melons

THE BOTTOM LINE

The soup was cold, the salad was wilted, and the fish was overcooked. When the waiter handed Mr. Essen the bill for his meal, Essen wrote on it

and strode out of the restaurant. Can you figure out what this meant? (Hint: It was not his American Express number.)

TAKE AN EDUCATED GUEST

Here's a sporting way to ease your guests from the den to the dining room. Give each person a pencil and a piece of paper on which you've written the numbers 1 through 20, with a blank above each number. Read aloud the following questions, and ask your guests to write the appropriate letters beside the proper numbers.

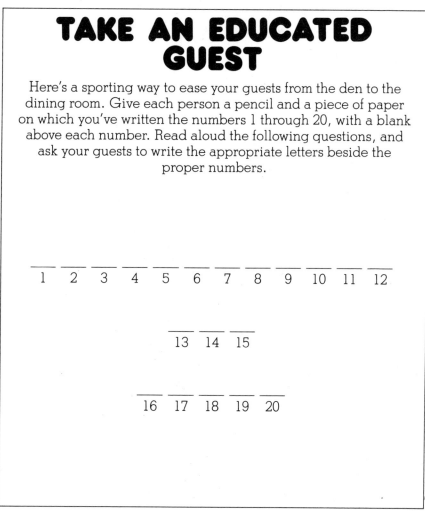

$\overline{}$ $\overline{}$ $\overline{}$ $\overline{}$ $\overline{}$ $\overline{}$ $\overline{}$ $\overline{}$ $\overline{}$ $\overline{}$ $\overline{}$ $\overline{}$
1   2   3   4   5   6   7   8   9 10 11 12

$\overline{}$ $\overline{}$ $\overline{}$
13 14 15

$\overline{}$ $\overline{}$ $\overline{}$ $\overline{}$ $\overline{}$
16 17 18 19 20

1

If your nephew's grandfather is your grandfather's son, write R in spaces 1, 4, 14, and 16.

2

If Y comes before H in the alphabet, write Z in space 3. If it comes after H, write F.

3

If 145 is more than 12 dozen, write E in spaces 2, 5, 9, 15, and 17.

4

If you like ice cream better than mosquitoes, place S in spaces 6 and 12. If not, see your doctor at once.

5

Closing one eye and not counting on your fingers, write the eighth letter of the alphabet in space 7.

6

If Dante wrote "Mary Had a Little Lamb," write O in space 20. Otherwise, write Y.

7

If *asleep* and *awake* are opposites, write M in space 8. If you're asleep, never mind.

8

If eight quarts make a pint, draw an elephant in space 10. Otherwise, write N.

9

If ice cream is more fattening than—well, let's not go into that. Just write D in space 19 and T in space 11.

10

Finally, if you think this is absolutely silly and you're dying for something to eat, write A in spaces 13 and 18, and follow me.

ANY WAY
YOU SLICE IT

A large pizza
is always delivered
cut
into eight slices.
But when our pizza man
is in a good mood, he tosses
in something extra—
a piece
from another pie.
If you can reconstruct
the eight-piece pizza
by matching sausages,
pepperoni, mushrooms, and
other fixings
along the edges,
you'll be able to spot
the extra piece.

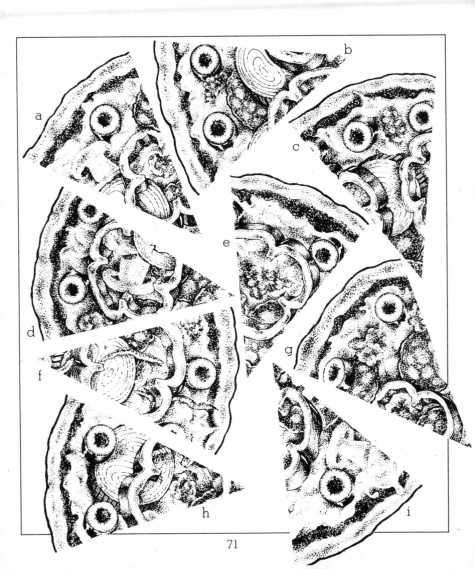

WANNA BET?

This bar bet falls into the puckish prank category, and is particularly effective in front of a crowd. You and the butt of the bet will each need four matchsticks, a cork, and a shot glass filled with any beverage. Bet your friend that he can't duplicate every move you make. Just follow the sequence described below, being careful to proceed with the next step only after your friend mimics your previous one.

1
Move one match forward.

2
Move another match forward and place it at a right angle to the first one.

3
Move a third match forward to form the third side of the square.

4
Take the last match and complete the square.

5
Hold your glass up and pour the contents into your mouth, snapping your head back.

6
Place your empty glass upside down on the bar.

7
Place your cork inside the square.

8
Pick up your empty glass, turn it over, and squirt your drink back into it. Your friend, having of course swallowed his, will not be able to duplicate that move.

ELASTIC APTITUDE TEST
PART III: SCIENCE

In each group, choose the one item that does not belong with the other four. Be prepared to defend your choices.

1
a) celery b) pineapple c) strawberry d) persimmon e) currant

2
a) condor b) raven c) flamingo d) heron e) piranha

3
a) fir b) chrysanthemum c) cypress d) beech e) yew

4
a) deer b) dog c) flea d) wolf e) rat

5
a) sand b) rock c) Princess telephone d) water e) soil

CHOCOLATRIVIA

Chocolate. Even the word is delicious, three toothsome syllables that conjure up mouth-watering associations. Chocolate eclairs, German chocolate cake, Godiva chocolates, chocolate fudge brownies. . . . If you find it hard to get through the day without one of the above, this quiz is just your cup of cocoa. It's guaranteed to lead you to deeper, richer insights into the things you love. Reflect. Ruminate. Unwrap your favorite candy bar. And begin.

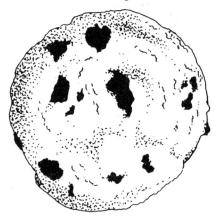

1 Suppose you start out to make chocolate-chip cookies by opening a 12-ounce bag of Nestlé's Semi-Sweet Morsels, but instead you end up eating them, one by one. When the bag is empty, how many will you have eaten?
a. 350 b. 675 c. 900

by Steven Clar   74   Answers, page 153

2 What is the area of the foil wrapper from a Hershey's Kiss?

a. 5 square inches
b. 2 square inches
c. 1 square inch

3 If you unwrapped one to measure it, what did you do with the kiss?

a. ate it (all other answers unacceptable)

4 If you answered "a" to question 2, how many calories did you just consume?

a. 25
b. 50
c. 100

5 How many segments are there in a regular Hershey bar?

a. 12
b. 16
c. none—regular Hershey bars aren't divided into segments

6 The world's first chocolate-chip cookie was created when the proprietress of the Toll House Inn, in Whitman, Massachusetts, mixed small bits of chocolate into her cookie dough, expecting the bits to melt and an all-chocolate cookie to result. Happily, this did not occur. This historically delicious event took place in:

a. 1870
b. 1903
c. 1930

7 Chocolate-chip cookies account for 50 percent of all cookies baked in U.S. home kitchens. How many chocolate-chip cookies are home-baked each year?

a. 70 million
b. 700 million
c. 7 million

8 The color proportions of M & M's have been determined by consumer preference. In a bowl of 100 M & M's, how many are likely to be green, yellow, brown, red, orange, and tan?

9 The world's largest chocolate Easter egg took two weeks to construct and measured more than 10 feet high and 24 feet in circumference. How much did it weigh?
a. 484 pounds
b. 884 pounds
c. 4,484 pounds

10 One candy bar has remained the nation's favorite for years. Which one is it?

11 The largest seller at U.S. movie theater candy counters is
a. Goobers
b. Raisinets
c. Junior Mints

12 Which chocolate bars do each of the following slogans tout?
a. "Sometimes you feel like a nut, sometimes you don't."
b. "It's the great American, great American chocolate bar."
c. "Two great tastes in one candy bar."
d. "_ _ _ _ _ _ _ makes the very best chocolate."

13 How much chocolate do Americans consume in an average year, and about how much do we spend to satisfy this passion?
a. 2 million pounds; 4 million dollars
b. 4 million pounds; 2 billion dollars
c. 2 billion pounds; 4 billion dollars

14 True or false: Never trust anyone who doesn't eat chocolate.

GLUTTONS FOR PUN-ISHMENT

The appropriate response to a pun is not a laugh, but a groan or a moan or an ugh. When a pun is really, really bad, it's the top of the lion, pridewise. Like this one:

> The Boy Scout saluted smartly
> after he had repaired the horn
> on the little old lady's bicycle.
> "You know our motto!" he said,
> "'Beep Repaired.'"

For your puzzling pleasure, the punchlines in the following groaners have been replaced with blanks. Can you fill in the blanks for a good laugh?

1

If after you've washed your child, he goes and gets all muddy again, then shoving him back in the bathtub for a second scrubbing is making the punishment

_____ _____ _____.

2

During the reign of Alexander the Great, a special dye was discovered which, when put on a rag or a piece of cloth, would change its shade depending on the angle of the sun. This enabled people to tell the time of day. Of course, one of these dye-soaked materials was presented to the king. He wore it proudly, tied around his head. And that is the origin of

_____ _____ _____.

3

The Republic of China has begun to export its beer to North America under the stimulating brand name of

_____ _____.

4

An inexperienced butcher in northern Canada was asked to butcher and package a huge moose. Never having seen one before, the young man nonetheless managed to get it cut up and to parcel and label the obvious parts—steaks, chops, ribs, etc.
However, he had a lot of pieces left over that he couldn't identify. So he parceled them as well and marked each one
"_____."

5

One night a breeze came up while an orchestra was giving an open-air rendition of Shubert's Ninth Symphony. During the intermission, most of the musicians spent their time tying down their sheet music to their stands. However, the bass players simply went to a nearby lounge for a few drinks.
When the conductor returned to the podium, he was dismayed to find in the last half of the _____ that the scores were _____ and the basses _____.

6

Joan of Arc didn't quit. She was _____.

7

All ogres can be divided into three kinds: the good ogres, the bad ogres, and _____.

8

When the cannibal chief returned from a walk, he found his men had captured a member of the British nobility. The cook was busy preparing their guest for dinner.

"Why is there fruit in his mouth?" the chief asked.

"Because, sir," replied the chef proudly, "tonight I am serving

_____ _____ _____.

9

Usually unreliable sources claim that Humphrey Bogart and Pamela Mason were secretly in love but could never risk getting together in Hollywood because of gossip. Finally, Bogie saw their chance when he was going on location to film *The African Queen.* What could be more natural than an Englishwoman like Pamela going to Africa for some big game hunting?

On their first night together, Bogart was sitting in front of their tent smoking while Pam unpacked. Suddenly a huge lion sprang at them! In an instant, Pamela had the gun out and shot it.

As she bent over the animal, it began to stir.

Bogie took a drag on his cigarette and drawled,

"_____ _____ _____ _____."

10

When the CIA got President Thieu out of Vietnam, they put him up at an apartment in Paris where they had formerly housed Argentina's deposed president, Juan Perón.

Fortunately for the CIA's budget, the rent for the apartment had not increased since Perón lived there, proving that

_____ _____ _____

_____ _____ _____ _____.

PASS YOUR BODY THROUGH A POSTCARD?

In spite of all the puzzles you've devoured
in this chapter,
you'll still be able to squeeze your body
through this paper-cutting trick.
It's an old chestnut that sounds outrageous,
but is actually very easy to perform.

Fold either a postcard or an index card
in half lengthwise, and make cuts as indicated in diagram 1.
(The exact number is not important,
but the more the better.)
Make your first cut from the creased side,
your second from the open side, and continue alternating,
never cutting all the way across from either side.
The last cut, like the first,
should begin from the creased side.

Then unfold the card and cut along the crease
(as shown by the dotted line in diagram 2),
stopping about one-quarter of an inch from both ends.
Now you can stretch the card into a large circle,
pass your body through it,
and collect on your bets.

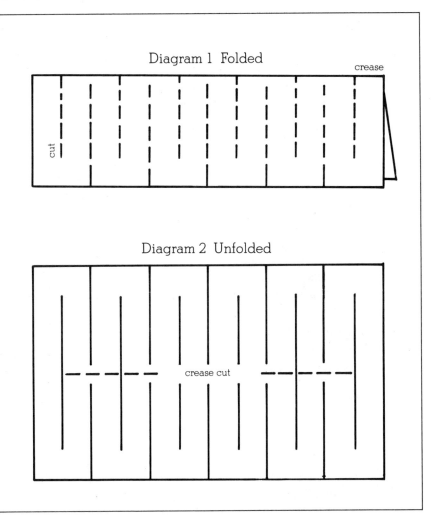

Diagram 1 Folded

crease

cut

Diagram 2 Unfolded

crease cut

Can you name
10 items
of footwear
that begin with
the letter S?

MAKIN' TRACKS

Who are the owners of these famous footprints?

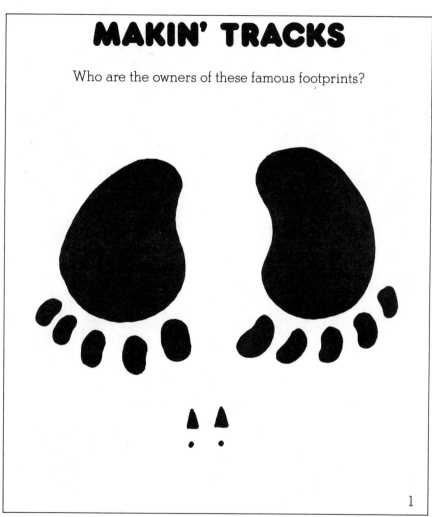

1

2

3

4

5

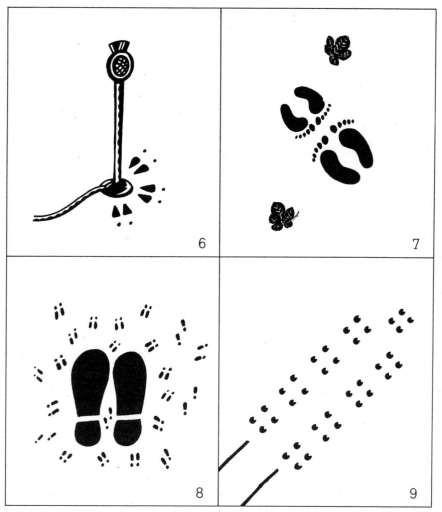

6

7

8

9

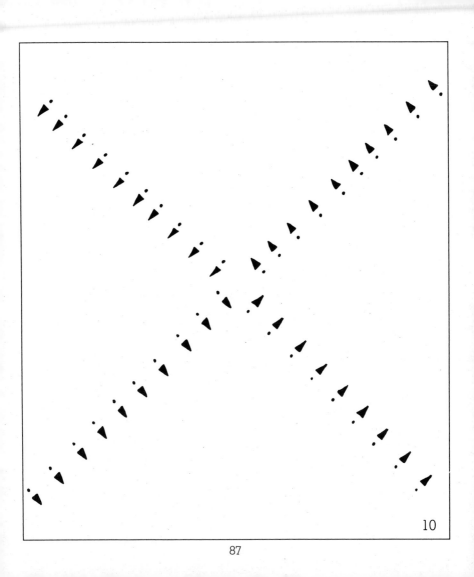

10

11

12

DANCIN' FEAT

All the questions below refer to dances and dancing, so put on your thinking cap and your dancing shoes and get ready to boogie.

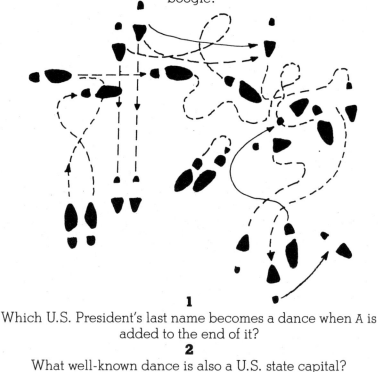

1

Which U.S. President's last name becomes a dance when A is added to the end of it?

2

What well-known dance is also a U.S. state capital?

3

Riddle: What was the Richmond projectionist's favorite dance?

4

If you spoonerize (swap the first sounds of) BALLET SHOES, you get CHALET BOOZE, which might be defined as "wine of the Swiss Alps." Name a dance which, when spoonerized, sounds like "a sour-tasting whiskey bottle."

5

A common measure of time becomes a dance when its last two letters switch places. What's the dance?

6

Rearrange the same seven letters to form common words that make sense in the following sentence.

Phooey! We can't dance the __ __ __ - __ __ __ __ until the busboy who dropped the __ __ __ __ __ __ __ cleans up the __ __ __ __ __ __ __!

7

GIVE A TOSS... WAY UP IN THE AIR... COME BACK DOWN
No, these aren't dance instructions for Baryshnikov and his partner. Each of the three phrases defines a common word. When the three words are rearranged correctly (no mixing of letters is involved), they spell out a lively two-word dance. What is it?

8

When you remove the first and last letters from the name of a famous dancer, you're left with a common word that means, appropriately enough, "step." Who's the dancer?

PLAYER PIANOS

Never mind what this piano arrangement sounds like—all that matters is what it *looks* like. Below are four overhead views of a disconcerting arrangement of 15 grand pianos. Only one of the four exactly duplicates the arrangement on the facing page. If you're really sharp, you'll find it in nothing flat.

a

b

c

d

FRANKLY, MY DEAR

Frank Sinatra seems to have a song for every occasion. Which of his trademark standards would he sing . . .

1
To a dermatologist
2
To a sadist
3
To NASA
4
To a poltergeist
5
After a big disappointment
6
At the circus
7
To a mule
8
To a female hobo
9
About Nancy, Ava, Mia, and Barbara
10
On the Staten Island Ferry

ELASTIC APTITUDE TEST PART IV: MUSIC

Answer the following questions in complete sentences. Students who know their song lyrics should score high.

1

In what portion of the Iberian peninsula is the mean annual precipitation the greatest?

2

In the absence of suspended atmospheric particles, what are the limits of visibility?

3

What migration was undertaken by the grizzly, and why?

4

Did a Supreme Being create small, underripe fruit?

5

What shocking discovery has NASA been keeping from the public?

6

What sound is made by the ermine?

7

What prayer did the bandleader utter on July 4?

8

If the sun were to rise in the west and set in the east, what could fairly be said?

9

Why are the aphids so happy?

10

Why can't you answer this question?

ROCK'N'ROLL REVIVAL

The Fillmore North presents a week of rock'n'roll music with some of the very best groups from the 1960s and 70s. There are seven big shows—Monday through Sunday night—with two bands playing each show. From the rebus-like posters created to promote the festival, can you identify the 14 bands?

97

ARIA READY FOR THIS?

The popularity of opera—grand, not soap—
has grown tremendously in recent years,
thanks to its frequent exposure on television.
More people may see *La Bohème* in a single telecast
than have seen it in all the opera houses of the world combined
since it was composed. This multiple-choice quiz
was designed to help you find out what you
(know, think you know, don't want to know) about opera.

1

The premiere of Verdi's *Aïda* took place in (Rome, Hoboken,
Cairo). The heroine, Aïda, is a (courtesan, slave, fan dancer)
who dies tragically with her love in a (low dungeon,
high dudgeon, curmudgeon).

2

In *Carmen,* the most famous opera by (Bellini, Belafonte,
Bizet), the heroine is (strangled, stabbed, thanked) by her lover
(Don Giovanni, Don Ho, Don José) because she has run off with
a (cavalry officer, flamenco dancer, bullfighter).

3

Puccini's *Tosca,* composed in the style known as (vermicelli,
verismo, vino bianco), concerns Floria Tosca, a (singer,
barmaid, mermaid), who is in love with a (sailor, painter,
gondolier) and who is almost seduced by a (U.S. Navy
lieutenant, police chief, political terrorist). She sings the aria
("La donna è mobile," "Pizza! Pizza! Mio Dio!," "Vissi d'arte"),
after which she (kisses, stabs, drowns) her would-be seducer.

4

Maria Callas, the soprano who revived the singing style called (prima donna, belladonna, bel canto), was born in (Athens, New York, Peoria) and was once married to (Aristotle Onassis, Giovanni Meneghini, George Papadopoulos).

5

In Gounod's *Faust,* the title role is sung by a (tenor, bass, halibut). Faust trades his (worldly goods, soul, liver) to the (Devil, king, IRS) in return for (youth, three wishes, a weekend with Goethe). But ultimately he wants to trade it back because he loves (Cher, Brünnehilde, Marguerite), who is eventually redeemed through the intervention of (Henry Kissinger, angels, Mephistopheles).

6

Although Mozart was born in (Germany, Austria, Tel Aviv), his opera *Don Giovanni* is sung in (German, Hebrew, Italian). The don is a (liberal, libertine, librarian) who kills the (father, husband, canary) of a woman he is trying to seduce and, in the end, is destroyed by the victim's (curse, statue, masseur). Mozart's first name, by the way, was Wolfgang; his middle name was (Affidavit, Amadeus, Amonasro).

7

Wagner's "Ring," a cycle of (4, 5, 12) operas, concerns the perilous adventures of (Tristan, Siegfried, Kermit), whose parents were (bats, Valkyries, brother and sister). He falls in love with (Sue Ellen, Cio-Cio San, Brünnehilde), the (first, last, ugliest) woman he ever saw.

8

The total number of operas composed by J. S. Bach, Chopin, Brahms, Paganini, and Beethoven is (1, 4, 7).

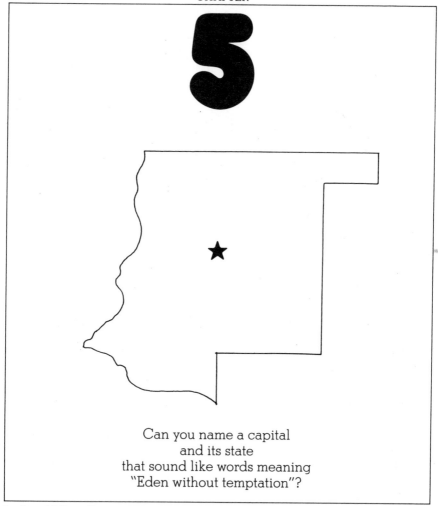

Can you name a capital
and its state
that sound like words meaning
"Eden without temptation"?

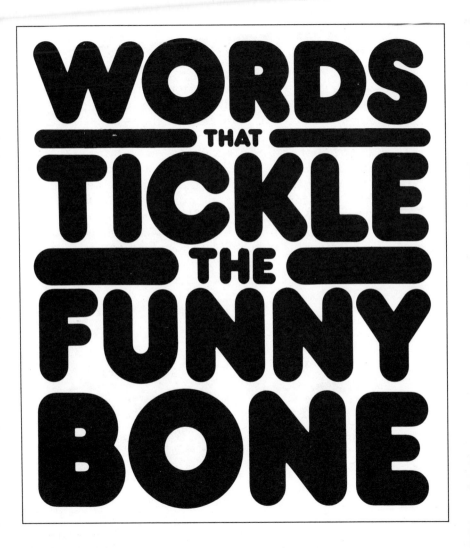

WORDS THAT TICKLE THE FUNNY BONE

CARTOONERISMS

The Reverend William A. Spooner, warden of New College, Oxford, in the first quarter of this century, earned a place in puzzle history through his charming errors of speech. "Spoonerisms" are words or phrases in which the initial sounds are transposed, as in "blushing crow" for "crushing blow." Each pair of illustrations on these and the following two pages suggests what has come to be called a spoonerism. By correctly choosing two words to name the first picture in each pair, then switching their initial consonant sounds, you will get a spoonerism for the second picture. In the example below, picture "a" is a *sinking wheel;* switch the S and W sounds and you will easily identify picture "b" as a *winking seal.* Got it? Then toe goo it!

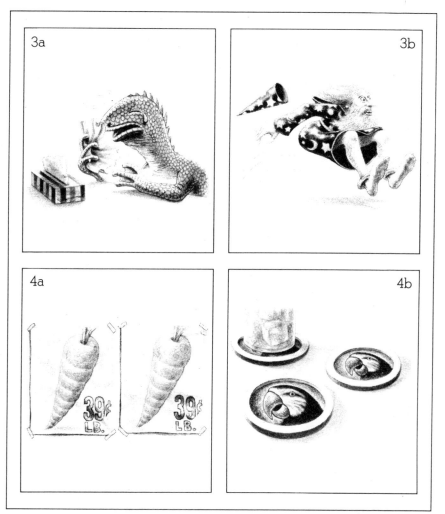

5a

5b

6a

6b

SO I SAYS...

Forget about grammar.
"So I Says" is a game
in which a given statement
must be humorously completed
by an appropriate first name.
For example:
*So I says to the girl standing
in the swamp, I says Marsha...*
In the sentences that follow,
fill in the blanks
where the names should be.

1
So I says to the girl blessing the food, I says _____.
2
So I says to the fellow floating gently on the waves, I says

_____.
3
So I says to the girl taking me to court, I says _____.
4
So I says to the man seasoning the soup, I says _____.
5
So I says to the guy using the PA system, I says _____.
6
So I says to the lady drinking Harvey's Bristol Cream, I says

_____.
7
So I says to the chap changing his tire, I says _____.

8

So I says to the man learning to tame lions, I says

_____.

9

So I says to the guy getting dressed, I says _____.

10

So I says to the woman making hamburgers, I says

_____.

11

So I says to the fellow saying his prayers, I says _____.

12

So I says to the boy doing subtraction, I says _____.

13

So I says to the two guys with the drums, I says _____.

14

So I says to the girl watching the sunrise, I says _____.

15

So I says to the kid playing with his trains, I says _____.

16

So I says to the fellow who lost 20 straight poker hands, I says

_____.

17

So I says to the man headed to phys. ed., I says _____.

18

So I says to the girl at the beach, I says _____.

19

So I says to the woman learning Morse code, I says

_____.

20

So I says to the chap who won the lottery, I says _____.

EXCUSES, EXCUSES

On Monday morning, seven students brought in written excuses
for not having their homework. Their teacher, having found all
the excuses unsatisfactory, cut them into one-word pieces and
then sketched a series of dashes and stars on a large sheet of
paper. "Here's an assignment," she told the students.
"Put these excuses back in their proper order—
and the starred letters will spell out the only reason
I'll believe for not turning in your work."

Excuse Words

A A I I

BY DO IN IT IT IT IT IT IT MY MY MY MY MY ON ON TO

AND AND GOT HER OUR THE THE

CAGE FIRE LEAD SOLD WITH WITH

LINED POKED UNCLE

CAUGHT MOTHER MOTHER MYSELF PENCIL SISTER
SMOKED

CHICKEN GARBAGE ROOSTED WRAPPED

COCKATOO HOMEWORK

FIREPLACE GIRLFRIEND POISONING

Excuses

1 __ __ ___ ___ __ ___ ___ ___ __
  *   *

___ ___ ___ ___ ___ ___ ___ ___
              *

___ ___ ___ ___ ___ ___ ___ ___ ___.
        *   *

2 __ __ ___ ___ ___ ___ ___ ___
     *   *

___ ___.

3 __ __ ___ ___ __ ___ ___ ___
  *   *   *

___ ___ ___ ___ ___ ___ ___ ___.
  *   *

4 __ __ ___ ___ __ ___ ___ __.
                       *

5 __ __ ___ ___ ___ ___ ___ __
       *   *   *

___ ___ ___ ___ ___ ___ ___ ___.
                          *

6 _ ___ ___ __ ___ ___ ___ ___
  *   *

__ ___ ___ ___ ___ ___ ___
        *   *

___ ___ ___ ___ ___ ___ ___.
        *   *

7 __ __ ___ ___ __ ___ ___ ___
                      *

___ ___ ___ ___ ___ ___ ___ ___

__ __ __ __ __.
        *

FOREIGN ACCENTS

If a Hindu benefactor
is an
Indian giver,
what
would
you
call
each of
the people
described
below?

1
An Iranian toupee
2
A gossip from Thailand
3
A Teutonic farmhand
4
A Scandinavian buffoon
5
Señor Yul Brynner

ELASTIC APTITUDE TEST
PART V: GEOGRAPHY

A good sense of direction may or may not be helpful in this quiz. Your task is to interpret each statement so that it becomes false.

1

Rome is the capital of Italy.

2

The Poles may be found in Warsaw.

3

The Nile is longer than the Danube.

4

The highest point in Asia is Mount Everest.

5

Turkey's temperature never exceeds 100° F in November.

6

Oslo is *not* located in the middle of Czechoslovakia.

7

Man can be found on every continent.

SAY IT WITH FLOWERS

Recently, this question rose: Mayflowers leave one laughing?
We'd been garden a stock of puns for quite some time, and took
this question as an opportunity to pick out a few daffy dillies.
Simply fill the blanks with flowers of the proper length,
one letter per blank.
Thistle probably be a quiz that provides a yucca two. But acacia
not tickled pink, well, that's just the way it gorse . . . .

1

Why did Buddy __ __ __ __ __ __ __ __ __ his guitar?

2

"Is that player a Detroit __ __ __ __ __" __ __ __ __ Tomlin inquired?

3

"Silence is __ __ __ __ __ __" __ __ __ Serling once said.

4

It's a __ __ __ __ __ __ __ __ __ __ __ __ a heavy load if you've got a good donkey pullin'!

5

Heaven's exciting, but I find __ __ __ __ __ __ __ __ __ .

6

I like Count Basie, Dizzy Gillespie, and other __ __ __ __ __ __ __ __ .

7

I __ __ __ __ __ __ for a kiss and she gave me a smack!

8

The moon's pull makes the __ __ __ __ __ in tides.

9

How often did __ __ __ __ __ __ __ __ __ __ __ cloak for his Dracula role?

10

I've gotten a lot __ __ __ __ __ __ __ __ __ I drank that gin!

11

"Ha __ __ __ __ __ __ body seen my gal?"

12

Do you remember Satchmo singing that great old tune "__ __ __ __ __ __ __ __ __ __?"

113

FUNNY BUSINESS

If big businesses lived up to the promise of their company names, you might expect Sunkist to make tanning lotion. Here are some other goods and services that certain companies might provide if their names were a literal indication of their business. Can you match each hypothetical product with a real corporation?

1. Jump ropes

2. Calendars

3. Home cookware

4. Bottled gases

5. Bird cages

6. Providing part-time trainmen

7. Boxing gloves

8. Outdoor grills

a. Goodyear

b. Pan American

c. Sears

d. National Semiconductor

e. Wham-O

f. Weyerhaeuser

g. USAir

h. Swingline

HOW MANY?

How many
answers
can you
find
to fill
in the blank
in the
following
sentence
so that
it is
true?

THIS SENTENCE HAS _____ LETTERS.

WHAT DO YOU GET WHEN YOU CROSS...?

Each of the odd-looking beasts on these six pages is a hybrid of
two familiar animals. The name of each hybrid is formed by
phonetically combining the names of the two parent
animals—that is, the beginning of one parent's name and the
end of the other's. For example, number 1, the offspring of a
mouse and a lobster, is called a "mobster." The description
of each animal (in number 1, "Runs in a gang")
gives a clue to its name. Can you determine the parentage and
the name of the other animal hybrids?

1. Runs in a gang

2. Appears to be very wise

3. Has a very rich fur

4. Was born in early October

6. Is very fond of wine

5. Is very lazy

7. Lives in groups, military style

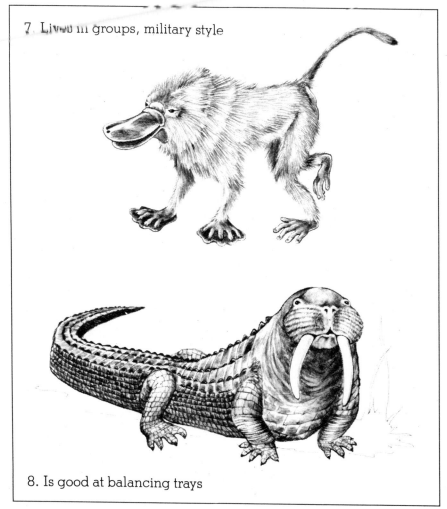

8. Is good at balancing trays

9. Has a sweet disposition

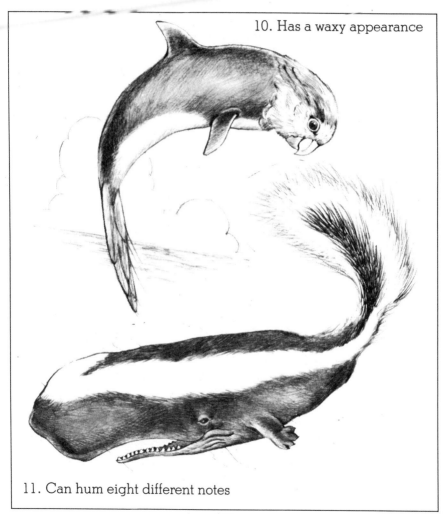

10. Has a waxy appearance

11. Can hum eight different notes

VERBAL TENNIS

Amid the brilliant repartee in Tom Stoppard's play *Rosencrantz and Guildenstern Are Dead* is a clever word game that R & G call "questions."

The game—which has a certain cult following,
especially on college campuses—
is sometimes renamed, more descriptively, verbal tennis.
Two opponents volley questions back and forth;
a player scores a point
when his opponent fails to return his volley,
that is, when the opponent responds
with a statement or a foul.
A foul is defined as
(1) a non sequitur, that is,
something that does not follow logically
from what has previously been said;
(2) a repeated question; or
(3) a rhetorical question
(one that does not require an answer).
Three points wins a game, two games wins a match.

Herewith, a few sample volleys.

X: Shall we play tennis?

Y: Who starts?

X: Why do you want to know?

Y: Doesn't it affect the game?

X: Did you think it would affect the score?

Y: Oh, are we keeping score?

X: How else would one of us win?

Y: I don't know!

X: Statement! One-love. Shall we continue?

Y: This is harder than I thought.

X: Statement! Two-love. Are you learning from your errors?

Y: What difference does it make?

X: Don't you want to improve your game?

Y: Who cares?

X: Foul! Rhetorical question! Three-love. First game to me.

Y: So, what was the score?

X: The score of what?

Y: Weren't you watching the ball game before?

X: Which ball game are you referring to?

Y: Didn't the Mets just play Montreal?

X: Are you interested in the Mets now?

Y: Didn't you know I'd given up on the Yankees?

X: Does that mean they have no fans left?

Y: Is it hot in here because your fan's broken?

X: Foul! Non sequitur! One-love.

Y: What do you mean, non sequitur?

X: Huh?

Y: Foul! No grunts! One all . . .

If you decide to play at home, be warned: The game, like
tennis itself, requires lots of practice.
Are you ready to begin?

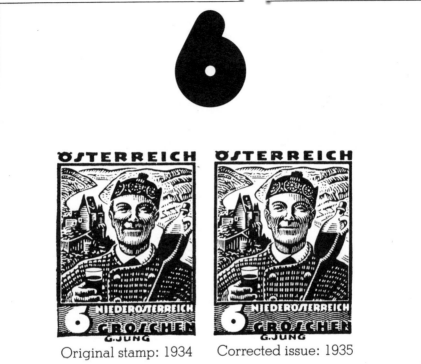

Original stamp: 1934   Corrected issue: 1935

The postage stamp on the left, issued in Austria in 1934, has a single error that was corrected the following year. By comparing the two stamps, can you tell what's wrong with the original?

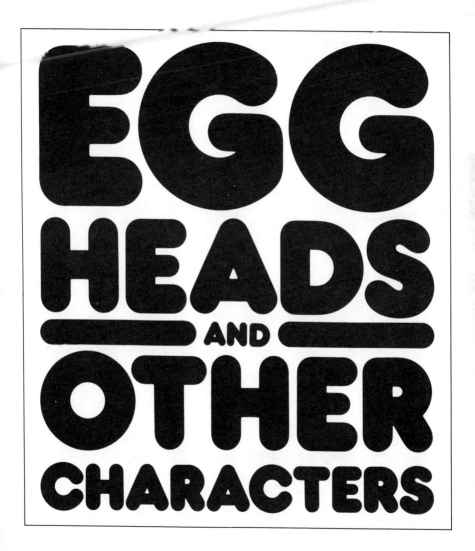

DISINHAIRITED

Some students of evolution think the
human race is slowly evolving toward
hairlessness. We've already shed the
furry look of our Neanderthal
ancestors, and it may be that the
baldies among us are the forerunners
of our hairless future.

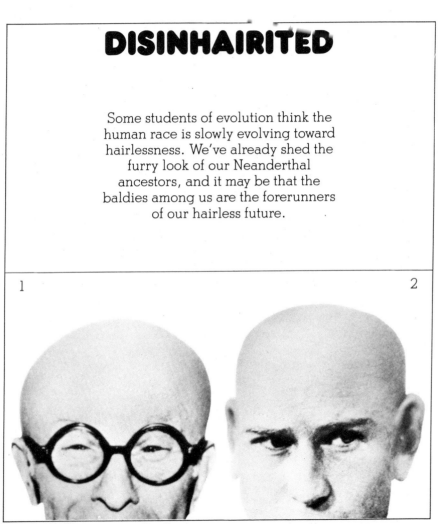

1

2

This puzzle speeds up the evolutionary
process by showing 12 celebrities with
shiny domes in place of their usual
coiffures. The faces are familiar...
do you recognize them?

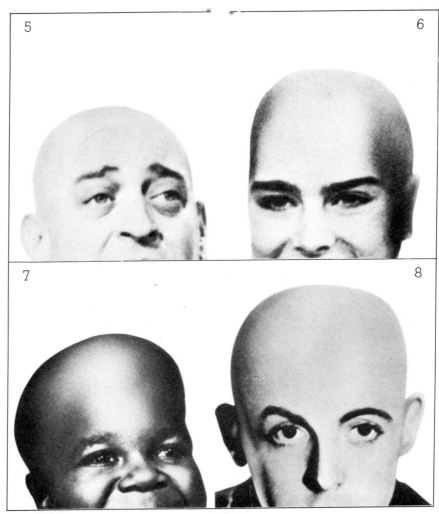

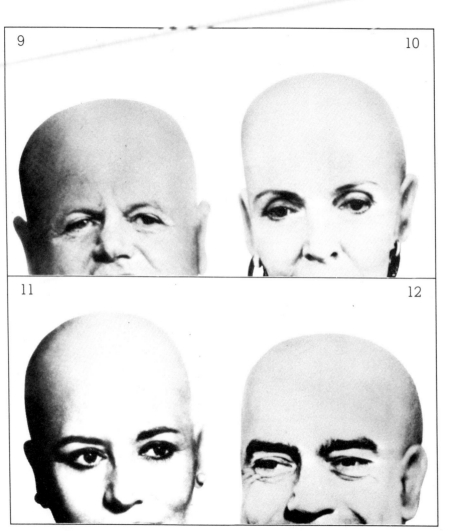

129

CALL OUR BLUFF

An untrustworthy soul by the name of Jeremy Piltdown presented us with this file of news clippings labeled "Strange and Remarkable Occurrences." Jeremy's object is to confuse the real world with the imaginary by providing equally bizarre examples of both, thereby proving that truth is often stranger than fiction. Can you determine which of these stories report events that really happened, and which are figments of Jeremy's imagination?

HITTING STRIDE

The novelist James Michener wrote his 800-page bestseller *Hawaii* without benefit of a plot outline and in a single continuous draft without corrections over a seven-week period on a manual typewriter. The rough draft was never revised by the author before submission, and the copy editor confessed he could find no reason to make a single change in the manuscript. The typesetter's galleys were accepted without corrections, and the first edition of the finished work contains no typographical errors.

You Only Go Around Once

Le Havre, France—Ulysse, a wily Belgian sheepdog belonging to a family here, strayed onto a transatlantic ship headed for Halifax in 1903. When he arrived there, he was identified by the nametag on his collar; but while arrangements were being made to ship him home, he escaped from custody.

He was successfully apprehended, albeit briefly in each case, in Toronto and Whitehorse in 1904, Nome in 1905, Vladivostok in 1908, Kabul in 1912, Karachi and Berlin in 1913, and finally again in Le Havre in 1915, where his arrival was greeted with great celebration. He has not left home since.

A DIFFICULT PATIENT

Ibsen himself spent the last six years of his life unable to write, staring out of his window in Christiania.

One day when a nurse announced that he was feeling better, the old curmudgeon found the ultimate putdown. "On the contrary!" he said, and died.

Whale of a Tale

St. John's, Newfoundland—While being rendered for spermacetti at an oil-processing plant here, a 14-ton gray whale dramatically exploded, spraying large chunks of blubber throughout the factory and forcing it to close for two months. While the mess was being cleaned up, three unexploded German torpedoes were found partly digested in what was left of the whale's stomach.

LIEBESTODT

Married: Moses Alexander, aged 93, to Mrs. Frances Tompkins, aged 105, in Bata, N.Y., on June 11, 1831.

They were both taken out of bed dead the following morning.

TRAFFIC

In 1895 there were only two cars in the whole state of Ohio. They collided.

INVESTIGATE BEFORE YOU INVEST

The result of a door-to-door survey of five thousand typical Americans was reported by *Collier's* in May 1949. Asked what was bought and sold on the New York Stock Exchange, 64 percent replied, "Livestock."

Mrs. Czermak's Descent

Prague—Vera Czermak jumped out of her third-story window when she learned her husband had betrayed her.

Mrs. Czermak is recovering in the hospital after landing on her husband, who was killed, the newspaper *Vecerny Pravda* reported today.

WALKING IRON MINE COLLAPSES

Tobata, Japan—A bet made several years ago finally caught up with 51-year-old Otoichi Kawakami last night.

Mr. Kawakami had convulsions and fainted in downtown Tobata. He was rushed to a hospital where surgeons removed from his stomach 13 safety razors complete with blades, 21 nails, a fountain pen, a pencil, 56 toothbrushes, 20 chopsticks, a piece of wire netting, and part of the ribs of an umbrella. He said he had swallowed the assortment on a bet several years ago.

Near Louisville, Kentucky, a rabbit reached out of a hunter's game bag, pulled the trigger of his gun, and shot him in the foot.

MOLISH JOKES

In the world of ethnic jokes, people tend to overlook the less visible minorities. Moles, for example, are entitled to their fair share of discrimination and are quite willing to ease the pressure on the more blue-blooded minorities. We'll introduce the genre with a few examples, and then see if you can guess the punchlines to the jokes that won the GAMES Molish Jokes Contest.

Q. What is the name of the best-selling Mole cookbook?
A. *Roots*, by Alex Moley.

Q

What is a mole made out of?

A

Molecules.

Q

How did the lady mole feel after attending Erhard Seminars Training?

A

Mole*sted*.

Q

How did the revolutionary mole overthrow society?

A

By using Moletov cocktails.

1

What are two occupational hazards of moles?

2

What is the favorite magazine of mole housewives?

3

Why aren't molish team sports popular?

4

What do you call the life-style of a mole who lives in a field of salad seasoning?

5

Why does the mole oppose the metric system?

6

What do you get when you mate a mole with a steer?

7

What do the common moles call the ruling class of moles?

8

What's the difference between a mole journalist and a mole tailor?

GROUND HOG MAZE

On Groundhog Day, all
the news teams and
camera crews want to
catch the little
critter on videotape
for the evening's broadcast.
But the groundhog
thinks, "Who needs
this?" All he
wants to do is peek
outside, see if he
has a shadow, and then
go back to sleep in his
den. How can he get
from the lower left
corner of the maze
through the tunnels
to the one hole that
isn't staked out by reporters?

by Robert Leighton

Answer, page 158

VITAL STATISTICS

She has posed for photographs and illustrations, been the butt of political satirists, and represented untold numbers of American products. As a national symbol she is ubiquitous. But how much do we really know about the Statue of Liberty?

1 Should Miss Liberty ever need glasses, the frames would measure about how far across?
a. 4 feet
b. 8 feet
c. 18 feet
d. 18 yards

2 Beauty is only skin deep. How deep is that, in the case of Liberty's copper skin?
a. 3/32 inch
b. 1/2 inch
c. 1 inch
d. 1 1/2 inches

3 The statue's weight is equal to that of
a. 32 elephants
b. 6 sperm whales
c. 475 horses
d. either a, b, or c

4 Were the statue ever to tire of being on a pedestal, and to climb down and check out the gift shop, how high would the doorway have to be for her to enter?
a. 59.2 feet
b. exactly 100 feet
c. just over 150 feet
d. 305 feet 1 inch

5 In 1918, our men in uniform at Camp Dodge, Iowa, posed in patriotic formation for this photograph.

How many men were in the picture?
a. 900
b. 1800
c. 9000
d. 18,000

COULD THEY HAVE...?

There's no end to the omissions in traditional history texts. This quiz should help fill in some gaps.

1
Could Dante have worn spectacles while writing
The Divine Comedy?

2
Could Davy Crockett have shaved with a safety razor?

3
Could Carl Sandburg have danced the twist?

4
Could Babe Ruth have signed autographs with a ballpoint pen?

5
Could George Frederick Handel have used a tuning fork?

6
Could Napoleon's armies have used dynamite?

7
Could Queen Victoria have ridden in an elevator?

8
Could Abe Lincoln have put up a barbed-wire fence?

AUNT HILDEGARDE

When we last saw Aunt Hildegarde, she'd been to see Aunt Louella, and had come home liking cinnamon but not curry, Beethoven but not Brahms, bikinis but not wetsuits. That's because our dear Aunt Hildegarde likes things that have the same word structure as the name of the relative she has seen most recently. And Louella, cinnamon, Beethoven, and bikinis are all words that have one letter repeated three times. This time, Aunt Hildegarde has been to visit Uncle Frank, and has come back home with a whole new set of likes and dislikes.

She shows EMOTION, but never PASSION.

She prefers CROOKS to CRIMINALS.

When playing Monopoly, she'd rather land on PARK PLACE than BOARDWALK.

Her favorite month is MARCH, and she doesn't like APRIL.

She loves WHOLE WHEAT BREAD, but not PUMPERNICKEL.

When it comes to ancient history, she prefers the GREEKS to the ROMANS.

She just bought a GRAY FOX COAT instead of a CHINCHILLA JACKET.

Can you figure out what guided Aunt Hildegarde's tastes on this visit?

WHAT A CARD!

Many magicians can read minds across great distances. Dick Cavett can't. But he can read *cards* across great distances—even ordinary playing cards. Get a deck and he'll prove it with this trick.

Shuffle the cards well. Holding them face down, turn over the top card and place it face up on the table. Imagine that its face value represents the number of cards in a stack, and deal face up on top of it as many more cards as needed to make a stack of 10. For instance, if it's a 3, deal seven cards on top of it; if it's a 5, deal five cards. Face cards count as 10, so no more cards are needed to finish their piles. An ace counts as 1 and needs nine more cards.

Continue making stacks of 10 as above, keeping the stacks separate, until the deck is exhausted. If there are not enough cards to complete the final stack, keep that incom-plete stack in your hand. Now choose, at random, any three stacks that contain at least four cards each and turn these stacks face down. Gather all the remaining cards in any order and keep them in your hand. Pick any two of the three face-down stacks on the table, turn up the top card on each of them, and add their values together. Discard that many cards from those in your hand, then discard 19 additional cards.

Count the number of cards remaining in your hand. Now turn up the top card on the third stack. Don't tell me what its value is, because I already know it. In fact, I've written it down in the answer section!

SYMBOL-MINDED COMPUTERS

Computers are so sophisticated that it may be only a matter of time before they will be able to think on their own. S½eptics don't believe this will ever happen. How can anything made of silicon wafers and microchips ever ac)uire the ability to thin½ and reason?

There's no dou&t that computers are intelligent and versatile. They can instruct, sol:e, play games, and e:en set t#pe. In fact, a computer printe@ these lines #ou are now rea@ing. &ut it's too much to e/pect that a com%uter will act on its o__n an@ ;ust ma½e changes at __ill.

Sometimes com%uters seem almost human. The# can as½ for @ata or tell us __hen an error has &een ma@e, as if there is a li:ing, thin½ing entit# &ehin@ the metal an@ %lastic faca@e, ;ust __aiting to e*erge.

If ¢o*%uters ¢oul@ tal½ to us it __oul@ %ro&a&l# &e in %rint, using s#*&ols instea@ of letter$. &ut $in¢e ¢o**uni¢ation i$ i*%o$$i&le . . .

"Hello, *# na*e i$ Zagron. I a* a ¢o*%%'ter. I ha:e t__o)'e$t!on$ = or #o'. __hat are t¼e $!/ (etter$!n t¼e$e %aragra%¼¼4$ t¼4at ! @!@ not ¢on:-rt + o $#*&o($, an@ __¼4a+ @o+ ¼4-# $%-((?"

ELASTIC APTITUDE TEST PART VI: ESSAY QUESTION

Write your essay here.
Be sure to maintain a concise style.
Print legibly, and remember
that spelling counts. _____

Can you cut the Q
into three pieces
that can be rearranged
to form the A?
The pieces may be rotated,
but none
should be flipped.

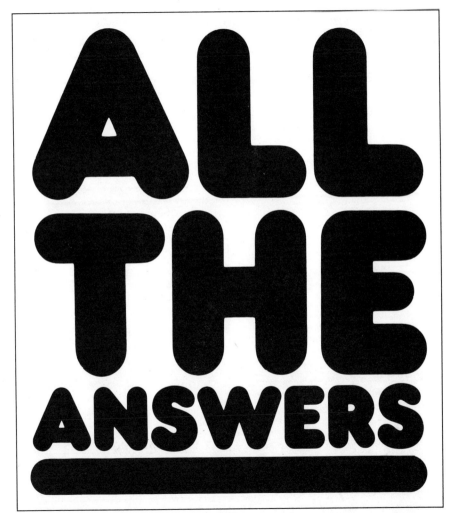

6 WHAT DO THESE ITEMS HAVE IN COMMON?

They all possess head parts: An airplane has a nose, a bottle has a neck, a clock has a face, and a comb has teeth.

8 ONE NEVER KNOWS, DO ONE?

If you thought the answers were—

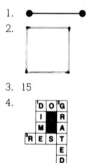

1.
2.
3. 15
4.

—you were half right. Now can you find another solution to each question?
Answers, page 154

10 DROODLES

1. Man in tuxedo who stood too close to the front of an elevator
2. Famous scientist seen through a microscope
3. Four elephants inspecting a grapefruit
4. Two bugs making love in the spring
5. An elephant hang-gliding (by E. L. Bland)
6. Bird's-eye view of a flagpole (Marla Raff)
7. A quarter on its way into a piggybank (Karin Dickson)
8. A voltwagon pulling a mobile ohm (Linda Wilson)
9. A fat man doing a handstand (Pat Reinken)
10. The bottom view of a diver on a diving board (David Morrison)
11. Nun listening to headphones (Peg Chandler)
12. Converted rice (Shawn McNamara)
13. Partial eclipse of a sesame seed bun (Peter Wortmann)
14. Abe Lincoln voting (Gail Withers)

The two examples, and numbers 1–4, are by Roger Price, the author of *Droodles #1* (Price/Stern/Sloan). Droodles copyright © 1953 by Roger Price. Numbers 5–14 are by the winners of the GAMES Droodles Contest.

16 THREE TEASERS

1. Eight—seven passengers and the bus driver.
2. The plane is sitting on the ground in Denver, a.k.a. "The Mile-High City."
3. It is noon. The clock must be wrong.

17 UNCOMMON EQUATIONS

5 fingers + 5 fingers = 2 hands
1 day − 60 minutes = 23 hours
3 quarters + 5 nickels = 1 dollar

18 TIC-TAC-TOE

The winning line, the diagonal reading from lower left to upper right, shows a "tick," a "tack," and a "tow"! This intended answer was not the only one—if you know Hebrew. GAMES reader Robin Asaki submitted this alternate solution: The octopus (bottom center) has eight tentacles, the center square has the word "eight" in it, and the Hebrew word for pen (top center) is pronounced "ate."

20 ELASTIC APTITUDE TEST PART I: MATH

1. All the choices are correct:
   (a) $3 + 6 = 9$; $4 + 6 = 10$
   (b) $3 \times 3 = 9$; $4 \times 3 = 12$
   (c) $3^2 = 9$; $4^2 = 16$
2. The probability is a certainty. Two objects of *any* kind form a pair.
3. εL
4. All are divisible by 3, yielding the respective quotients $11\frac{1}{3}$, $9\frac{2}{3}$, $18\frac{1}{3}$, 34, and $2\frac{1}{3}$.
5. Give yourself half credit if you said 9, 11, 13 to continue the series of odd numbers. Give yourself full credit if you said 8, 9, 10 to continue the series of positive integers whose names contain the letter E.

22 WACKY WORDIES

1. Trafalgar Square
2. Eggs over easy
3. Pie in the sky
4. Turn over a new leaf
5. Growing pains
6. Total loss
7. Little League
8. Sitting duck
9. Double or nothing
10. Bottomless pit
11. Four-wheel drive
12. *Twice-Told Tales*
13. Swear on a stack of Bibles
14. Bridge over troubled water
15. Set one's teeth on edge
16. Negative attitude
17. Power blackout
18. Flip Wilson
19. Trial separation
20. Lying down on the job
21. Prosperity is just around the corner
22. Counter-clockwise
23. Turn of the century
24. Writer's cramp
25. Checkout counter
26. Between-meal snack
27. Shopping center
28. Unfinished business
29. Bet one's bottom dollar
30. Mixed metaphor
31. Not up to par
32. Headless Horseman
33. Yield right of way
34. Repeating rifle
35. High school
36. What goes up must come down
37. *The Price Is Right*
38. Abridged dictionary
39. Pizza with everything on it

28 WHAT ARE THE RULES OF THIS PUZZLE?

A correct interpretation of the convoluted rules reveals that the answer is the name of the puzzle—"What are the rules of this puzzle?"—and the number 24 (obtained by multiplying the numbers of paragraphs 4 and 6).

The correct numbering of the six paragraphs of rules, in order of appearance, is: 3, 2, 5, 6, 1, 4. Paragraph 1 (all paragraph numbers here refer to the numbers just listed) states, "The last sentence in the next-to-last paragraph of these rules is to be ignored," and also makes it clear that for this purpose "next-to-last paragraph" means paragraph number 5 (rather than paragraph 1, which appears next-to-last on the page). The sentence to be ignored is therefore the second one in this key paradoxical statement: "If two sentences in the same paragraph contradict one another, follow the one that comes last. But if two sentences in the same paragraph contradict one another, follow the one that comes first." Thus whenever two statements within a paragraph are contradictory, the second statement is to take precedence. Once this is deduced, the rest is (relatively) straightforward.

30 SPORTS QUIZ

1. c
2. (a) The quarterback is throwing a basketball instead of a football, and there is no 60-yard line on a football field.

(b) Julius Erving is dribbling a soccer ball instead of a basketball, and his number is 6, not 8.
(c) The pitcher is tossing a football instead of a baseball, and the fence should read *ft.*, not *yds.*
(d) The hockey player is skating with a baseball instead of a puck, and the referee in the background isn't wearing skates.

32 FROM THE FLIMFLAM FILE

1. It stands for Explain The Meaning Of This Acronym.
2. The letter P is in the middle of THE ALPHABET.
3. In
4. The blind man said, "I'd like to buy a pair of scissors."
5. The hat was hung on the end of the gun.
6. You would prefer that the lion ate the tiger.
7. NEVER ODD OR EVEN is a palindrome, reading the same backward and forward.
8. Bet on 5. The die is probably loaded.
9. Horse racing and horseshoes
10. Change post to p-o-s-t.
11. Unusual
12. 7g = b (Most people write 7b = g.)
13. None. Noah built the ark.
14. "Damn it, can't you see I've got my mouth full of nails?"
15. This question will be answered in a future book.

34 LIP READING

Top row, from left: Matthew, Alfred, Eastman
Second row: Richard, Theodore, Luke, and Oom
Bottom row: Hisswald, Shirmer, Fletcher, Arthur, and Alden.

36 SATE WITH SCOTCHOGRAMS

1. I'm never as happy as I am when I'm with you dear. Love and kisses.
2. Can you spend this weekend with us in the country? Wire the minute you know.
3. Do not bet on the race horses. A word to the wise is sufficient.
4. I'll be at the track. You never said if I must have a ticket to get in.
5. When the house caught fire, Sy had to come out of doors in just his socks and shorts.
6. We're returning this order since the sizes are wrong.
7. We'd like a nice chest for our mother. The sky's the limit.
8. Can't sell my old car to you. It's in for malfunction.
9. You're in a fix. Lost your case. You're going to jail. Can serve ten years. You ought to appeal.
10. Bob's still at sea. Can't anchor his boat. You must go to him or tell the Coast Guard.
11. I let Sheila into your house. She lost her key.
12. Mary's in bed. She hurt her knee. A gust of wind knocked her into the brush.
13. Why don't you send me the names so I can fill out a list?

Scotchograms came our way via a 1928 book by Jack Shuttleworth, *Say It with Scotchograms* (John Day Company). The first three puzzles are from that book; puzzles 5 and 6 are from the winners of the GAMES Scotchogram contest (Bruce W. Niedt and Diane Davis respectively); the others are by the GAMES editors.

38 EYEBALL BENDERS

The objects are:
1. Skillet
2. Phone
3. Net
4. Ax
5. Sander
6. Key
7. Knife
8. Oar
9. Pick (guitar pick)
10. Jars

The rebus message is "Skill at phonetics and a keen eye for pictures."

40 BO'S BEAUS' BOWS

1. Fore for four
2. Knew new gnu
3. Weigh whey way
4. Pare pear pair
5. Rein rain reign
6. Write rite right

41 WILLIAM MARRY ME?

1. Matthew
2. Walter
3. Arthur
4. Annie
5. Florence
6. Dwayne

42 MARRIED WOMEN

1. Sarah (Miles) + (Ralph) Nader
   = Serenader
2. Ida (Lupino) + (Don) Ho = Idaho
3. Rose (Kennedy) + (Billy) Budd
   = Rosebud
4. Belle (Starr) + (Timothy) Bottoms
   = Bell-bottoms
5. Bo (Derek) + (Danny) Kaye
   = Bouquet
6. Bea (Arthur) + (Christopher)
   Reeve = Bereave
7. Lindsay (Wagner) + (David) Doyle
   = Linseed oil
8. Anna (Freud) + (Franz) Liszt
   = Analyst

44 CARTOON REBUSES

1. Gemini
2. Tripoli
3. Robinson Crusoe
4. *St. Elsewhere*
5. Marcel Marceau
6. Kuwait
7. Willie Mays
8. Labor Day
9. "Que Sera, Sera"

48 SH-BOOM!

1. "Charlie Brown"
2. "The Witch Doctor"
3. "Tutti Frutti"
4. "Why Do Fools Fall in Love?"
5. "The Name Game"
6. "He's So Fine"
7. "Imagination"
8. "Get a Job"
9. "Breaking Up Is Hard to Do"
10. "I Met Him on a Sunday"

49 AD INFINITUM

1. The American Express
   Card—Don't leave home without it.
2. Let your fingers do the walking
   through the Yellow Pages.
3. Good to the last drop. (Maxwell House)
4. Put a tiger in your tank. (Esso)
5. Plop plop, fizz fizz, oh what a relief
   it is. (Alka-Seltzer)
6. When you care enough to send the
   very best. (Hallmark)
7. Reach out and touch someone.
   (Bell Telephone)
8. Have you driven a Ford lately?
9. Fly the friendly skies of United.
10. Aren't you glad you use Dial?

50 BLPS

Five blops are neither blips nor bleeps.

51 SIMPLE ADDITION

The total is 4,100, though 9 people out of 10, when solving aloud as directed, come up with an answer of 5,000.

52 OMPHALOSKEPSIS IS EASY

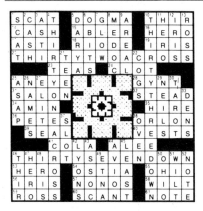

54 HOW'S THAT AGAIN?

The lower court ruled that the owner did not have the right to fire a waiter for serving (refusing to deny service to) a male patron not wearing a tie and jacket. This ruling was overturned by the appellate court, which was upheld by the Supreme Court's first ruling but reversed on rehearing. Thus the lower court's original ruling stands. Since a waiter may not be fired for serving a male patron without a tie and jacket, such a patron is likely to be served.

Jack and Jill are first cousins. Jill's mother's sister is Jill's aunt, and the aunt's son-in-law is the husband of Jill's cousin. The cousin's maternal grandfather is also Jill's grandfather, whose wife is Jill's grandmother. Grandma's son John is Jill's uncle (not her father, since in that case Jill's parents would be brother and sister), and John's son, to whom the book is being returned, is therefore Jill's cousin.

Bill will be facing north.

55 ELASTIC APTITUDE TEST
PART II: LATIN

1. (f) good dog
2. (a) a good rental car is hard to find
3. (d) ambulance
4. (g) dirty poem
5. (c) Freudian self-actualization
6. (e) change your psyche
7. (b) see the janitor

56 WHAT'S NEW?

The correct order of the panels is d, g, b, a, e, c, f.

58 CONFUSABLES

Emily Brontë wrote *Wuthering Heights,* Charlotte wrote *Jane Eyre* (and sister Anne wrote *Agnes Grey*). Electrons are negatively charged. And Alaska was admitted to the Union before Hawaii.

1. Romeo was a Montague and Juliet a Capulet.
2. + to + and − to −
3. *Titanic,* iceberg; *Lusitania,* U-boat
4. Stalactites hang from the ceiling.
5. Plato was a student of Socrates.
6. Warp (woof is the filler thread)
7. Right (left is port)
8. Bronze (brass is copper and zinc)
9. John Rolfe
10. Apogee, highest; perigee, lowest
11. *Monitor,* Union; *Merrimac,* Confederate
12. Ophthalmologist (An optometrist examines for and prescribes correctional lenses, and an optician grinds the glass for them—whew!)
13. Lower
14. Four pecks make a bushel.
15. Right to left

62 A PEAR-PLEXING PROBLEM

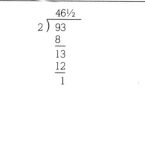

$$
\begin{array}{r}
46\frac{1}{2} \\
2\overline{)\,93} \\
\underline{8} \\
13 \\
\underline{12} \\
1
\end{array}
$$

64 SUBSTITUTIONS ALLOWED

1. Greene	17. Glass
2. Mellon	18. Wilde
3. Black	19. Rice
4. Bean	20. Shepherd
5. King	21. Bacon
6. Crabbe	22. Burger
7. Lake	23. Rolle
8. Cooke	24. Brown
9. Shore	25. Blue
10. Schell	26. Berry
11. Fish	27. Pound
12. Cole	28. Lemmon
13. Cobb	29. Sellers
14. London	30. Coco
15. Dunne	31. T
16. Sothern	

66 POETRY IN THE KITCHEN

1. (g) Grenadine for the queen
2. (j) Fudge for the judge
3. (c) Lox for the jocks
4. (a) Mints for the prince
5. (i) Kasha for the pasha
6. (d) Plums for the bums
7. (b) Leeks for the sheiks and chives for their wives
8. (f) Crabs for the scabs
9. (k) Melons for the felons
10. (h) Liquor for the vicar and buns for the nuns
11. (e) Granola for the Ayatollah

67 THE BOTTOM LINE

1 0 2 0 0 4 1 8 0 = I ought to owe nothing for I ate nothing.

68 TAKE AN EDUCATED GUEST

The result reads REFRESHMENTS ARE READY.

70 ANY WAY YOU SLICE IT

Slice f is the odd piece out, and the only one with anchovies. The other slices fit together (in clockwise order) as follows: a, g, d, c, e, i, h, and b.

73 ELASTIC APTITUDE TEST PART III: SCIENCE

1. (a) Celery is the only word that does not have a doubled letter.
2. (e) Piranha does not make a new word when its last letter is removed.
3. (b) Chrysanthemum does not have a homophone (a word that's spelled differently but pronounced the same).
4. (c) Flea does not form a word when read backward.
5. (c) Princess telephone cannot be used as a verb.

74 CHOCOLATRIVIA

1. (b) The actual count is about 675, but our author has eaten his way up to only 542.
2. (a) After having undressed many Kisses, we find the average wrapper to measure 2¼ x 2¼ inches—an area of about 5 square inches.
3. (a) Unless, of course, you fed it to someone else.
4. (a) According to the Hershey Foods Corp., an ounce of milk chocolate contains 150 calories. Since six Hershey's Kisses weigh one ounce, each Kiss is worth 25 calories.
5. (a) Several such bars were sampled in our research, to make sure there were no discrepancies in the number of segments per bar.
6. (c) According to the Nestlé Company.
7. (c) And that's almost enough to eat one's way to the moon!
8. 40 brown, 20 yellow, 20 orange, 10 green, and 10 tan. Red M & M's were discontinued in 1976. (Sorry for the red herring.)
9. (c) The 1980 *Guinness Book of World Records* reports that this wondrous feat occurred in Victoria, Australia, in 1978.
10. Snickers, according to the National Candy Buyers Brands Survey.
11. (b) Raisinets
12. (a) Almond Joy and Mounds, respectively
    (b) Hershey Bar
    (c) Reese's Peanut Butter Cups
    (d) Nestlé's
13. (c) According to the Chocolate Manufacturers Association of the U.S.A.
14. Undeniably true.

8 ONE NEVER KNOWS, DO ONE?

1. • *shortest possible line* •

2.
   (Four *is* a "perfect square!")

3. 3 (The sequence refers to the number the minute hand points to every 15 minutes on a clock.)

4.

	C	U	R	
	E		A	
	N		S	
S	T	O	P	
			E	
			D	

77 GLUTTONS FOR PUN-ISHMENT

1. Fit the grime
2. Alexander's Ragtime Band
3. Taiwan On
4. Mooselaneous
5. Ninth . . . tied . . . loaded
6. Fired
7. Mediogres
8. Duke a l'orange
9. Slay it again, Pam
10. Thieu could live as cheaply as Juan

The puns are reprinted from *The World's Worst Puns* by John S. Crosbie (Harmony Books, 1982).

82 ON YOUR FEET!

Sandals, shoes, skates, skis, slippers, sneakers, snowshoes, socks, spurs, and stockings, among others.

84 MAKIN' TRACKS

1. King Kong and Ann Darrow (Fay Wray)
2. Charlie Chaplin
3. The Incredible Hulk
4. Hansel and Gretel
5. Alice Through the Looking Glass
6. The Andrews Sisters
7. Adam and Eve
8. Gulliver and the Lilliputians
9. Santa Claus and his reindeer
10. The Rockettes
11. Tiny Tim
12. Captain Ahab or Long John Silver

90 DANCIN' FEAT

1. Polk (polka)
2. Charleston
3. The Virginia reel
4. Jitterbug (bitter jug)
5. Minuet (minute)
6. Two-step, stewpot, wet spot
7. Highland fling
8. Astaire

94 FRANKLY, MY DEAR

1. "I've Got You Under My Skin"
2. "Try a Little Tenderness"
3. "Fly Me to the Moon"
4. "I Don't Stand a Ghost of a Chance With You"
5. "That's Life"
6. "Send in the Clowns"
7. "I Get a Kick Out of You"
8. "The Lady Is a Tramp"
9. "Love and Marriage"
10. "New York, New York"

92 PLAYER PIANOS

The answer is d, which has been rotated 90° clockwise.

Based on a puzzle from the Canadian magazine *La Magie Des Jeux*.

95 ELASTIC APTITUDE TEST PART IV: MUSIC

1. "The rain in Spain stays mainly in the plain."
2. "On a clear day you can see forever."
3. "The bear went over the mountain . . . to see what he could see."
4. "God didn't make little green apples."
5. "It's only a paper moon."
6. "Pop goes the weasel."
7. "Don't rain on my parade."
8. "It's a most unusual day."
9. "Everything's coming up roses."
10. "It's impossible."

96 ROCK 'N' ROLL REVIVAL

Monday:	The Temptations and Iron Butterfly
Tuesday:	The Doors and The Grateful Dead
Wednesday:	Led Zeppelin and Aerosmith
Thursday:	The Eagles and The Mothers of Invention
Friday:	Three Dog Night and Manhattan Transfer
Saturday:	The Who and The Electric Light Orchestra
Sunday:	The Rolling Stones and Cream

98 ARIA READY FOR THIS?

1. *Aïda* was premiered in Cairo. Aïda is a slave who dies with her lover in a dungeon.
2. In *Carmen,* by Bizet, the heroine is stabbed by Don José because she left him for a bullfighter.
3. *Tosca* is an example of the *verismo* style. Floria Tosca, a singer, loves a painter and is almost seduced by a police chief. She sings "Vissi d'arte" and stabs her would-be seducer.
4. Maria Callas, the reviver of the *bel canto* style, was born in New York and was married to Giovanni Meneghini.
5. The title role in *Faust* is sung by a tenor, who trades his soul to the Devil in return for youth. He loves Marguerite, who is saved by the intervention of angels.
6. Mozart was born in Austria. *Don Giovanni* is sung in Italian. The don is a libertine who kills the father of a woman he is trying to seduce and is destroyed by the victim's statue. Mozart's middle name was Amadeus.
7. Wagner's "Ring" is a cycle of four operas. Siegfried is the hero, the son of a brother and sister. He loves Brünnehilde, the first woman he ever saw.
8. Beethoven composed one opera (*Fidelio*), the others none.

100 STATE CAPITAL

We didn't think you could . . . but how about Annapolis, Maryland (an apple-less merry land)?

102 CARTOONERISMS

1a. Dripping wagon
1b. Whipping dragon
2a. Sore fox
2b. Four socks
3a. Weeping lizard
3b. Leaping wizard
4a. Carrot posters
4b. Parrot coasters
5a. Hand carts
5b. Canned hearts
6a. Wired tail
6b. Tired whale

Based on an idea by John Dart.

106 SO I SAYS . . .

1. Grace
2. Bob
3. Sue
4. Herb
5. Mike
6. Sherry
7. Jack
8. Claude
9. Don
10. Patty
11. Neil
12. Les
13. Tom . . . Tom
14. Dawn
15. Lionel
16. Mark
17. Jim
18. Sandy
19. Dot
20. Rich

108 EXCUSES, EXCUSES

1. I do my homework by the fireplace and it caught on fire.
2. A chicken roosted on it.
3. My mother wrapped our garbage in it.
4. My uncle smoked it.
5. My sister sold it to her girlfriend.
6. I poked myself with a pencil and got lead poisoning.
7. My mother lined the cockatoo cage with it.

Starred letters: I hate homework so I didn't do it.

110 FOREIGN ACCENTS

1. A Persian rug
2. A Siamese cat
3. A German shepherd or a Hamburger helper
4. A Swedish meatball
5. A Mexican hairless

111 ELASTIC APTITUDE TEST PART V: GEOGRAPHY

1. The letter I is the "capital" of Italy.
2. The Poles are at the extreme north and south of the planet.
3. It's shorter by two letters.
4. The top of the letter A is Asia's highest point.
5. It does, when roasted for Thanksgiving dinner.
6. Oslo is in Czechoslovakia.
7. No, man is an island.

112 SAY IT WITH FLOWERS

1. Hollyhock
2. Tiger lily
3. Goldenrod
4. Snapdragon
5. Hellebore
6. Jasmine
7. Aster
8. Sego
9. Belladonna
10. Hyacinth
11. Zinnia
12. Aloe Dahlia

114 FUNNY BUSINESS

1. (h) Swingline (jump ropes)
2. (a) Goodyear (calendars)
3. (b) Pan American (home cookware)
4. (g) USAir (bottled gases)
5. (f) Weyerhaeuser (bird cages)
6. (d) National Semiconductor
   (part-time trainmen)
7. (e) Wham-O (boxing gloves)
8. (c) Sears (outdoor grills)

115 HOW MANY?

We had three answers in mind when we originally posed the question in the magazine. Several readers looked a little deeper and came up with some imaginative alternatives, increasing the number of possible answers considerably:

1. THIRTY-ONE
2. THIRTY-THREE
3. 22
4. TEN and TWELVE if you count only different letters
5. XXV, XXVI, XXVII, or XXVIII (in Roman numerals)
6. THIRTY PLUS SEVEN,
   FORTY MINUS FOUR,
   NINETEEN TIMES TWO,
   or EIGHTY-SIX DIVIDED BY TWO

116 WHAT DO YOU GET...?

1. Mobster (mouse/lobster)
2. Guru (goose/kangaroo)
3. Tycoon (tiger/raccoon)
4. Libra (lion/zebra)
5. Loafer (llama/gopher)
6. Carafe (cat/giraffe)
7. Platoon (platypus/baboon)
8. Waiter (walrus/alligator)
9. Caramel (caribou/camel)
10. Paraffin (parakeet/dolphin)
11. Scale (skunk/whale)

124 WHAT'S WRONG WITH THIS POSTAGE STAMP?

The man's ears are on backwards!

126 DISINHAIRITED

1. George Burns
2. John McEnroe
3. Reggie Jackson
4. Bo Derek
5. Rodney Dangerfield
6. Brooke Shields
7. Gary Coleman
8. Paul McCartney
9. Ted Kennedy
10. Nancy Reagan
11. Barbara Walters
12. Dan Rather

130 CALL OUR BLUFF

The phony Piltdown stories are "Hitting Stride," "You Only Go Around Once," and "Whale of a Tale."

132 MOLISH JOKES

1. Trench mouth and tunnel vision (Susan Zivich)
2. *Better Holes and Gardens.* (Robert Griffin)
3. Moles only root for themselves. (W. F. Morris)
4. Living on burrowed thyme (Chuck Igou)
5. He heard it would do away with yards. (Jerry Bell)
6. Ground beef (Daryll Fickling)
7. A bunch of molarchy (Patrick Hurst)
8. None, they both work for the underground press. (Alex Dunne)

134 GROUNDHOG MAZE

136 VITAL STATISTICS

1. (b) Each eye measures 30 inches across and the space between her eyes measures 23 inches, for a total of 83 inches. Allowing a few inches on either side for stylish frames brings you to about 8 feet.
2. (a) 3/32 of an inch
3. (d) or about 225 tons
4. (c) 151 feet 1 inch, to be precise. The pedestal is 154 feet tall, so from the foot of the pedestal to the tip of her torch is 305 feet 1 inch.
5. (d) 18,000

138 COULD THEY HAVE...?

1. Yes. Alessandro de Spina of Florence (Dante's home town) is generally credited with the invention of "seeing discs" in Europe (c. 1286), although they were probably a Chinese invention. *The Divine Comedy* was completed c. 1321.
2. No. The safety razor was invented 67 years after Crockett's death at the Alamo.
3. Yes. The twist appeared in 1961. Sandburg died in 1967.
4. Yes. Although he had retired from baseball three years prior to the ballpoint's invention (1938), Ruth lived until 1948.
5. Yes. It was invented by one of Handel's orchestra's trumpeters in 1711.
6. No. Dynamite was invented by Alfred Nobel (founder of the Nobel Prize) in 1867.
7. Yes. The first passenger elevator was installed in a New York City hotel in 1859—more than four decades before the end of Victoria's reign.
8. No. Barbed wire was patented in 1874.

139 AUNT HILDEGARDE

Aunt Hildegarde likes words that become other words when the first letter is removed.

140 WHAT A CARD!

The value of the top card on the third stack is the same as the number of cards in your hand.

142 SYMBOL-MINDED COMPUTERS

Starting at paragraph three, here's the translation:

Sometimes computers seem almost human. They can ask for data or tell us when an error has been made, as if there is a living, thinking entity behind the metal and plastic facade, just waiting to emerge.

If computers could talk to us it would probably be in print, using symbols instead of letters. But since communication is impossible . . .

"Hello. My name is Zagron. I am a computer. I have two questions for you. What are the six letters in these paragraphs that I did not convert to symbols, and what do they spell?"

The six letters are A, G, N, O, R, and Z, and they spell the computer's name—ZAGRON.

143 ELASTIC APTITUDE TEST PART VI: ESSAY QUESTION

SA

144 Q and A

The cuts are made as shown below.

ACKNOWLEDGMENTS

In addition to the many individual contributors, it is the
editors of GAMES who provide the ideas, test the mechanics,
and iron out the kinks in the magazine pages where these
puzzles first appeared. Collectively known as Margot Seides,
they juggle sense and nonsense daily.
For their efforts on the book in hand, thanks to Don Wright for
his design, opinions, ideas, and solutions; to Robert Leighton
for suggesting funny sounds; to Lori Philipson
for copy editing, and to Toni Green for proofreading
and keeping track of things. Thanks also to Suzanne Rafer,
Julienne McNeer, and their colleagues at Workman Publishing
for getting the book from our hands to yours.

ILLUSTRATION AND PHOTOGRAPHY CREDITS

Page

6: Keith Right
18–19: Sandra Forrest
20: Dave Calver;
typography by Dave Herbick
31: Focus on Sports
38–9: Keith Glasgow
44–7: Kimble Mead
56–7: Robert Leighton
62: Sandra Forrest
71: Hal Just
74: Sandra Forrest
82: Sandra Forrest
84–9: Steven Max Singer

90: Sandra Forrest
92–3: James Forman
96–7: Sandra Forrest
100: Sandra Forrest
102–105: Greg Scott
112: Bryan Wiggins
116–21: Donna Ruff
126–29: UPI (1, 2, 5, 6, 9, 10, 11, 12);
Wide World (3, 4, 7, 8)
132: Mark Mitcham
135: Robert Leighton
137: Courtesy of Library of Congress
141: Courtesy of Dick Cavett